GET UNEMPLOYED

The Mindset, Business & Marketing Bible

by Graeme Lawson

Contents

ABOUT THE AUTHOR

I was a really happy kid. My mum says I was always smiling.

I wasn't exactly shy - sometimes in an insufferably boisterous way. I loved meeting people, making friends and trying to impress. Playing football, hide and seek, art, whatever - I was into it all.

When I went to school, I was very average academically and was definitely *'not cool'*.

Looking back through my old school report cards they **all** say the same thing, literally from my first year at 5 years old until I left high school at 17:

> *"Graeme is* <insert polite phrasing to describe average> *but he gets distracted too much… he talks too much."*

Although I was really happy and had great family, great friends in a regular working-class community - I was always hard on myself. I listened to everything my parents, my teachers, my friends, the people that gave me shit in school said and took it to heart. I was always a people pleaser.

I don't blame my mum and dad, like most good parents for thinking:

> *'If he dicks around, he's not going to get a good education, which means he's not going to fulfil his potential - which he'll regret later in life."*

All the while, this people pleasing from such a young age was shoehorning me into being this drone I knew my character wasn't. I felt like a weirdo and had to *'fix myself'* to fit in with everyone.

In high school, when you're 13 or so, you're expected to pick the subjects that define what you become when you're older. I remember vividly being stressed as fuck because I didn't know what the right answer was. When my parents visited the school guidance counsellor about it, his advice was to pick an array of subjects so I could *"go in any direction"*. I mean, Chemistry and Physics? I never even considered just picking what I **enjoyed**.

I was good at or enjoyed:

- Gym.
- Music.
- Art.
- Technical Drawing.
- Craft & Design (wood and metal work).

Know how many of those I picked?

Only gym.

Otherwise, which one of those was going to get me into a suit and tie, working 9 to 5, being a good little worker? I witnessed my dad working hard and being successful in an office job and figured that's where I'd end up.

After stumbling through high school, I continued to stumble through College and then University. Deliberately because both were on my doorstep and I was too lazy to think about my future, or too scared in case it was the wrong decision and I disappointed someone.

Then I dropped out of Uni.

I remember thinking the whole cycle was pointless. A basic education, yeah, but all the shit from the last 10 years? What a waste of time.

So, there I was, having stumbled through school, college, university and now stumbling from job to job. From shoe stores, to computer factories, to agency work and finally to a sales job that I was good enough at to make far more money than I was spending.

Years passed doing that - I enjoyed not being broke for the first time in my adult life and buying clothes and *'toys'* …but I still hated it. Being financially secure was all I had wanted, yet I wasn't happy. I hated the sales and I hated working for someone else with performance reviews, office politics, backstabbing, good natures being exploited …I didn't fit in.

So, in 2011 I truly pressed the *"Fuck It"* button and changed my life forever.

In the middle of the recession, with about 6 months (at most) savings in my bank, instead of putting that down as a deposit on a house and carrying on working a job I hated, against the advice of those around me and even my boss - I handed in my notice.

I'd threatened to start a business for about 6 years previously and never did it, but I'd reached breaking point. The smart thing to do would've been to build it on the side and carry on earning - but I knew I would half-arse it, not give it my full attention then probably give up or talk myself out of it.

I gave up my well-paid job and downgraded my car.

Jumping in with both feet was the only move. At least I could say I went for it. Quitting a well-paid job in a recession where I had no decent qualifications? The alternative of not knowing and always wondering *"what if"* was much worse.

I trained myself in what I wanted to learn, which was Web Design and Search Engine Optimisation (SEO), which is the ability to rank websites higher when a user searches for particular terms on a search engine – predominantly Google.

I did web design at college, but with the industry changing so fast, particularly around that time – I needed to re-train for much of it. It took around a month, but…

Money didn't exactly flow in right away like I'd hoped!

…so I had to go out and dig holes for my stepbrother's fencing business to make money (these pictures came up on Facebook for my 8 year *'On This Day'* recently).

As well as doing the fencing with my stepbrother I also got a weekend desk job at the local storage units.

Looking back, I also didn't take advantage of any of the fantastic support and funding this country offers ...but I guess you can learn from my mistakes.

It wasn't plain sailing once I got my first client either. Years went by and there were still months where no money came in because multiple clients didn't pay on time.

Fast forward 8 years and I've added way more strings to my bow in terms of the services I offer, my clients are also all on automatic payment systems and I've had an assistant for several years now. I've been involved in amazing projects and have transformed strategies for businesses large and small, growing them, making them more money and improving their systems and processes.

I travel: From seeing more of my own country, to around Europe, to 3-month stints in the likes of California and Thailand. I don't have an alarm clock and I work on my own terms.

Why am I telling you all of this? Because you need to know that whatever stage you're at in your life doesn't need to define you. The pressures to succeed at any age shouldn't consume you or stifle your creativity, personality or your ability to start and grow something.

The fact I get distracted and talk to people (the recurring theme in my school report cards), to enquire and learn about them, their lives, loves and motivations. The fact I'm extroverted and inquisitive in adulthood is a huge part of my success and makes me the person I am.

I was a little bitch and looking back I shouldn't have beaten myself up about it so much at the time. It's ok to be different because you don't fit the mould of a system building you into a 9 to 5.

Whatever happens, you'll be fine.

Go for what **you** want. It'll probably change a million times between the first thing you decide you want to do at 16 and by the time you're 25.

You might be 30+ 40+ 50+ and still just figuring things out.

It's never too late, time doesn't matter. What matters is your interest and your application in that interest. The application is easy when whatever that *'thing'* is interests you.

It's not the end until you give up.

Never give up believing in yourself or your goals.

WHY I WROTE THIS BOOK

A year ago I started typing out my thoughts. I like writing, I love philosophy and the study of human behaviour. The more I did it as a hobby the more I enjoyed it. That got me into the habit of writing about everything I was thinking, even the things that weren't just about my philosophy on life. I looked back after the year and realised I had **a lot** of notes. As I read through it all I realised:

"If I flesh this out, it could be a book!
…a book that's basically me in a nutshell, from all my honest notes to myself."

As I went through the notes I realised they all fell into at least one of three categories: **Mindset**, **Business** or **Marketing**. This book is the organisation of these notes into sections that are categorised to flow.

When I produced content in the past I was extremely careful and obsessed about covering every base, ensuring **everyone** liked it.

What I've learned is: No matter how good your content, no matter how honourable or well-intentioned it is – you're going to take shit.

Shit from those that:

- Don't know any better.
- Like the sound of their own voice.
- Never took a risk in their life and stand on the side lines giving you their *'wisdom'*.

Then there are other genuinely well-meaning people that just don't agree with you, which is fine (and useful).

If I were to write a book and 100 people read it, but 90% of the people don't get it, hate it, call it shit, are jealous, exist purely to troll or simply don't agree or think the swearing isn't for them – I'll meet 10 people that think like me, believe what I believe and want to work on themselves and their business with the same ethos.

Would you trade 90 people that don't like or *'get'* you for 10 people that do? You should - every single time.

You don't need to convert people. You need to find the people that are either already with you in their mindset, or consume your content and say:

"Man, I never thought of it that way, I love it!"

or

"This guy thinks like me - I should be doing this!"

My problem was I cared too much about being right for everyone. I always worried about the negativity - even though I **knew** if I had followed my own advice from the beginning of my journey I would be so much further ahead in both my mentality and my business.

I never put my voice out there and let likeminded people come to me. So that's what I'm doing now. It doesn't matter if more people dislike it than don't - being authentic is what's important.

The biggest courtesy you can give to someone or a group of people is being authentic.

Not how much you watch your language, not how nice you dress, not what you earn, not what you buy, not how true you are to social norms. Authenticity matters ...but it's in the minority - that's why it's so great when you meet someone else with similar values. Spend your time in both life and business meeting and working with those people that matter to you and share your values.

I'm finding likeminded people, and those are the people I choose to spend my time with, to be inspired by and have a beer with. Have you read the comments sections of any social media platform? Most are idiots anyway. Find your people and filter out the morons from your life.

As I began to write this, I wasn't sure how long it would be - I tend to write things succinctly and although I might repeat myself, I hate to waffle or labour a subject. Turns out it's actually much longer than I anticipated (well over 70,000 words), but its purpose is to inspire action in you and provide massive value. It's to help you understand what works on a mindset level, on a practical business level and how to market your product or service. It's to inspire aspiring and current business owners, from teens in high school, to retired couples, from single mums, to professionals looking to start their own firms.

We're not all cut out to be 9 to 5'ers and this book serves as a guide I wish I

had when I first started out.

I wasn't born an entrepreneur, I wasn't selling lemonade when I was 8, I wasn't selling football cards when I was 12 and I didn't start my first web design company at 16. Entrepreneurs aren't always born, I'm proof. I grew up in a small town and worked shitty jobs for the best part of my late teens and twenties.

Anyone can be a successful business owner, but not everyone wants it enough. Some won't take the risks, some won't accept the sacrifice, some won't persist. Some can't face the pain, the doubt and other people's opinions. Some are so afraid of others opinions that they never even start. But anyone reading this can factually be a successful business owner.

I'll teach you the actual mechanics, not just the theory or pictures on a beach, swinging in a hammock. With self-help, mindset or marketing books there's always too much of the *'dream scenario'*, not enough meat on the bones, but success **is** what happens when you take action and have persistence. **I'll show you how**.

People are sold on those online marketers that spend all of their time talking about the result, the beaches, the houses, the cars, the lifestyle - I was far more interested in the technical side; the actual mechanics of getting it done. That's why most of this book will focus on what to actually do and what will get you where you want to be - not just motivation and lifestyle. The mechanics are how you make the lifestyle stuff happen, otherwise you're just doing mental masturbation forever.

The same marketers, the so-called gurus, will typically make money telling other people how to run a business when they've never actually built anything tangible themselves. This whole:

"Oh hi, I was just pouring my morning coffee there…"

"I was just putting my kid to bed…"

"Look how relatable I am! <insert smiley emoji>*"*

Shut the fuck up and teach people something of substance.

I run marketing campaigns, grow companies and coach business owners on how to run their business better. I also help aspiring business owners start from scratch and market themselves effectively. I've been a freelance marketer and coach for over 8 years. I've been designing for at least double that. I **do not** make my money selling courses on how to make money, without having built anything myself.

It's a sad fact that many may dislike this book because it calls people out, pulls no punches and *'tells it like it is'*. There's infinite value in that, but some don't want to read it.

They want the cuddly:

"Everything is great, people are great, all you have to do is believe!"

"Turn your dreams into reality, follow your heart, you can do it!"

"Make your moon collide with your Sagittarius..."

If you mentally corrected that last one – I've got some bad news for you...

There's plenty of motivation in here, but it's never the cookie-cutter bullshit that makes you feel good for a day after reading it, only to go back to living the part of your life you wanted to change in the first place.

There's more money in selling the mindset to people. But mindset only allows people to stay in their comfort zone, and your comfort zone is not where things happen.

Learning all these aspects of marketing and applying it successfully for 8 years has allowed me to live where I want and explore any new ventures I want. You could probably learn everything I know about ...well ...anything in a few months. It's not the knowledge you need, it's the practice. You need to go out and do it.

You can read a book cover to cover, where every word and all the concepts makes sense...

You might understand it, but it's not until you take action, actually do it and internalise it through experience that you totally get it.

Once you start taking action, the experience you get effects the decisions you make going forward. Not in a cause and effect way, not in a learning from your mistake's way, but in the understanding of the entire ethos of what makes a successful business. Then, when a completely new problem or scenario unfolds where there's no guide book? You just **know** what to do.

Fall in love with the work, fall in love with the game and you'll never hate Monday again. You'll enjoy your *'working'* life so much more.

Understanding these principals and the marketing doesn't mean you can only start a marketing agency, either. Once you know these principals and take action - you can start just about any business!

"You can't blame everything on the economy, douchebag."
- Hank Moody, Californication

This book is about running a business, not with the help of anything else, but often **in spite** of everything else. The blame-game stops here and responsibility lands squarely at your door.

Do you tick a box and expect a politician to improve your life? Think again. The only one who needs to take responsibility is the person looking back at you in the mirror, and I'm here to help you do it. None of these excuses:

"I couldn't do it because of this or that."

"I have kids."

*"I have a degree and they won't **give** me a job."*

Get Unemployed and execute until you're the master of your own destiny. Employ yourself. Don't be reliant on anyone else giving you a job, or firing you, or making you redundant, or cutting your pay. Don't give anyone else the power, make your own decisions and...

Never again need anything so much that you can't walk away!

I'm not willing to sell my soul with this book. I know how to market it to get more sales, the sales funnels to use and sequences to sell more copies. However, if I only write one book, I want it to include everything I want to say and not have a series or sequels in mind. I want it to be 100% authentic, unconstrained by sales speak, false promises, mental masturbation or publisher structures and demands.

Over a year ago I started taking notes that I thought were only there to remind me whenever I got a little disillusioned, angry or side-tracked about why I do what I do. This book is the by-product of that.

When I got into business, all I wanted was freedom. Freedom from my alarm clock, freedom from playing the corporate game, freedom from a lunch break, freedom from asking if I can take holidays, freedom from consumerism, freedom from fakery, freedom from any geographical chains, freedom from quietly seeing out my life, freedom from painfully studying pensions and investments, freedom from wishing for something better.

I got it.

This book is all the best things I've learned through personal experience and studying. I want to help you achieve and bypass all the bullshit I had to go through. I don't have wanky abbreviations or exercises for you to do throughout the book – you just have to read it.

There's also a lot of sections that I feel don't get mentioned in other books or authors avoid through fear of upsetting the *'catch all'* nature of writing a book.

- This book is what I do for my clients.
- This book is what I coach others to do.

- This book is what I train people at speaking gigs.

I want to help and encourage people in their development because this shit should be shared with everyone - in fact it should be taught in school. It also shouldn't be hidden by those who have already achieved success and want it all for themselves, or apathy because they've done it and don't have motivation to pass it on.

"I'm all right Jack."

Is that acceptable? I don't think it is.

I hope you like this book - it's everything I've got to say so far.

MINDSET

FIRSTLY

Understand that your existence is pure chance.

This might seem overly deep for this kind of book, but once you understand the exact circumstances for:

- The world we live in existing in its exact form.
- The chances of **you** specifically existing.

Meaning your parents had to be those exact people, your mother had to get pregnant at that exact moment…

I mean, if your mum decided to stay in the night she met your dad or if your dad went to the game instead of staying in the night you were conceived …and for your parents' parents to have met and had that exact moment, and theirs, and so on, all the way back, before we evolved into humans, an unbroken lineage of over 4 billion years…

Your chance of existence is 1 in $10^{2,685,000}$
(that's a 10 followed by over 2 million zeroes)

Which is ultimately meaningless, except for the value you put on it yourself.

Why am I telling you this? Because overcoming fear of failure, worrying about what others think and fear of rejection stifled me all of my young life.

Putting this into the likelihood of your existence, nothing should stop you from trying and nothing should hold you back. Not caring what others think is one of the hardest things in life to master. It's instilled in us from such a young age - from watching those around us do it, to hesitating in school through fear of ridicule and anything else we're influenced by like our friends, our family and the media.

Other people's opinions are not important in the context of you setting your goals and following your dreams. It's where all the magic happens. Caring about what others think will only hold you back, and for what?

Remember, when anything sets you back or someone shits on your dreams and goals - the chance of your existence is basically zero…

Take it.

CRAB BUCKET MENTALITY

Before you start taking action on the Business and Marketing sections of this book, you need to understand Crab Bucket Mentality, as it can stop you any time you try to make a change.

Some people need a clear out (and I'm not talking about their house or their garage). Crab Bucket Mentality has affected us all at some point in life, and if you do nothing about it, it'll stifle everything you try to do that doesn't conform with what the masses want.

All the crabs in the bucket can escape with a little bit of effort, however, every time one tries to scale the wall of the bucket - the other crabs use their pincers and pull the escaping crab back in.

It's a metaphor for:

"If I can't have it, neither can you!"

This is not just for business. All of your life there will be people who tell you that you can't do things:

- Following a healthier eating plan and starting to lose weight?
- Going to the gym and visibly seeing muscular progress?
- Giving up alcohol?
- Changing careers?

There are those that, from the moment you mention a dream or a goal will try and talk you out of it, or give sarcastic, passive aggressive comments. Then there are those that seem supportive in the beginning …until you start to surpass their definition of success. They then feel threatened by your achievements. You're holding up a mirror to them, exposing their own inadequacies and insecurities.

Misery loves company.

The difficult thing about this is that it's often the people closest to you. It could be a parent, your partner, or your best friend. Sometimes it's someone we consciously know we shouldn't give a shit about, but we still let their words discourage us from pursuing what we want.

It is important to note however, that it's human nature. It's not actually personal to you, despite how it might feel. People are never going to be as happy for you as you are because they're always holding up that mirror, rarely seeing your attempts and achievements objectively.

If you're starting a business to gain plaudits, then don't start. When you first start out you might have a few encouraging voices that cheer you on, but the more you achieve and the more you surpass their definition of success the more jealous they get. The more they put the spotlight on themselves and hate that they aren't succeeding.

They hate that you came from a similar position in life to them and knowing a real-life example of someone who grasped the nettle and has the motivation and discipline that on refection they wish that they had - which is ridiculous!

They should be happy for you and understand the only person stopping them is themselves, but most people never get that far in their thinking. If you get nothing but joy in seeing someone else succeed and it inspires you to take action instead of jealously finding fault...

Congratulations - you're in a minority.

You'll see a direct correlation between those with this positive mindset and those that have success (or future success).

People will never stop trying to turn you into a drone. Passion and excitement in children is abundant. Do you have any idea how rare it is to see real passion in an adult? People say life beats it out of them, and some pretty terrible things can happen to a person, but you know it's mostly just other people chipping away at your character, passion and hope. Be glad you have things to be passionate about, instead of being a fake, boring drone. Don't listen to other people trying to belittle your enjoyment because the only things that pique their interest are trinkets and reality TV.

Crab Bucket Mentality features really early on in this book because it's one of the most important foundations that needs to be addressed before you even start. It's the hardest thing to rationalise; knowing consciously that you shouldn't give a fuck what people think, that the opinions of those that don't understand and have never taken a worthwhile risk in their life don't matter – but your subconscious still cares a great deal about it anyway.

Crab Bucket Mentality is something most people can battle with daily, depending on their environment - but it's important to understand the crab's behaviour so you can bust out that logic whenever you're taking shit from anyone.

LUCK

People interpret success with luck, when really - regularly taking action creates *"Luck"*.

People call me lucky. What part of giving up a well-paid job in a recession, eating noodles every night, working second jobs, or having no money because several clients haven't paid on time all at once, being alone with no instructions is *"Lucky"*?

Losers call others lucky because they don't understand life. They don't understand cause and effect.

It comes from lack of accountability. They like to use the term lucky as it excuses them from trying anything in case they *"weren't as lucky"*.

Taking opportunities isn't luck: Former Black Flag frontman Henry Rollins (who I admire hugely) tells the story about how he got started in his band. About how he got a *"Lucky Break"* to sing in the band that made him famous.

He explains how he was in a stable job in a rough neighbourhood where most people didn't even have jobs. He took the risk, gave up his job and moved state to try out for a band he always wanted to sing for. With his energy and tenacity, he got the job. He took the **risk**, he put in the **effort**, but he's still too humble and coins it *"Lucky"*.

Nothing about that story is luck! It's micro good decisions instead of a sea of bad ones he could've made.

It's important to start making decisions and taking risks that'll take you in certain directions. Directions can be good or bad, but there will be decisions that you look back on and say:

"Can you imagine where I'd be if I hadn't done that?!"

It's about the good decisions, even if you make more bad ones than good. Execute, make those changes and find out.

If my action creates 100 opportunities and I mess up 90 of them - I'm 10 opportunities ahead of the person who isn't even playing the game.

Maybe one of those 10 is a big contract I win, or an online business I start that makes enough money to retire at 40. People point to that and say:

"Ugh, he came up with an idea that happened to knock it out of the park first time - he's so lucky!"

Lucky? People that put minimal effort into everything attribute everything good in life to luck.

My luck is my mum, dad and brother are all healthy. My luck is that I got to meet all of my grandparents. My luck is that I was born in a western country with a stable upbringing. My luck is that I don't have anything genetic that's killed me yet. Those are my privileges, my things that make it easier - but it doesn't excuse you for not doing it if you don't have those things (except the death one).

There are never too few hours in the day to overcome your lack of privilege. Many in the same situation or worse have done it before you. No excuses.

The reason things happen are cause and effect, nothing more. Not god, not karma, not fate or *"The Law of Attraction"*. Cause and Effect.

"THE SECRET" WORKS!

For those that aren't familiar, The Secret is a famous book, which in turn became a motivational movie documentary about *"The Law of Attraction"*.

The idea is that by thinking positively and visualising your goal the *'universe'* literally gives it to you.

Sorry, *'Manifests'* it for you.

> *"You're the most cynical person I know, Graeme. There's no way you believe that shit!"*

Correct. It's all bullshit mumbo jumbo to trick people out of money. A way of taking something that genuinely works, sticking in a bunch of window dressing (that might as well be called *'magic'*) and making people pay for that knowledge.

Yes, it actually works …but not in the way the book and movie imply.

One star of the movie, a famous Law of Attraction type *"guru"* (who makes a fortune selling personal coaching, online seminars and live events teaching this stuff) actually uses the analogy in the movie that you don't understand how a light switch works, but you use it anyway - so the same principal can be said for The Law of Attraction.

Mate, you might not know how a light switch works, but other humans do, you know, with science! That pesky thing *"The Secret"* pretends to have a section on that really makes no coherent sense at all.

Thomas Edison didn't get round the campfire with his science buddies and *'wish'* to invent the light bulb.

It's a disingenuous disgrace to sell positive thought alone to cure your woes. Talk about keeping the poor, poor!

Here's why the law of attraction actually works:

"The words you speak become the house you live in."
- Hafez.

When you start to think positively, then let it consume your entire thought process on a particular goal - you can't help but move closer towards that goal. The actions you are now taking as a result of that thinking are what put you there. Cause and effect.

Furthermore, the more positive you are about a goal, the better decisions you make, the more you persist and the harder you try. It is pure cause and effect, nothing more.

You are not asking the universe; you are giving more brain-time to a goal in a more positive thought space. Your mindset is everything.

Law of Attraction gurus treat people like idiots, marketing to them saying *"the universe"* or *"you're like a magnet"*. As if it has to be packaged as some gimmick to sell to the masses. All it achieves in doing is making these shysters money!

Success is the cause and effect of your focus. Nothing more complicated than that and not the justification for a whole book or documentary movie full of made-up garbage.

You need to start thinking:

"No, fuck it - I'm going to go for this!"

Once you get out of your own way, quash the fears and just go for it - things open up for you.

It's not magic, it's not the law of attraction - it's cause and effect. What you're actually doing is reprogramming your subconscious. There are things in your head right now that stop you taking action, but I can almost guarantee you they won't be the reasons that it's either *'hard'* or *'can't be done'*.

There will be other genuine reasons that will surface and make it hard. Reasons that will come up when you start taking action, but they're never the insurmountable things you've built up in your head.

You know what happens? You fix those things, like any other aspect in your life. Don't dwell on things that 99% of the time don't happen, deal with the things that do come up and it will all come together. No exception.

I'll only backtrack by saying: If believing in whatever it is you believe **actually helps you**, then that is more important than me telling you it's bullshit. But people should not be making money overcomplicating it with pure, unadulterated theatre.

RISK

People are extremely risk averse. The fear of loss is always greater than any gain. It holds people back, stifles ambition, kills creativity and gives a skewed idea of achievability.

Nothing I've ever achieved was created without risk.

Risk is essential because risk equals reward.

When you start taking risks and seeing the rewards it reaffirms a new concept of risk. You understand the things that held you back weren't real, that all they did was make things longer to do, for no reason other than bullshit scenarios you concocted in your head.

"The problem is not the problem. The problem is your attitude about the problem."
- Captain Jack Sparrow

I'm so accustomed to risk that when I see someone deliberating over something so insignificant and petty with regard to risk - I realise how far I've come.

It's something you have to keep doing, keep on stretching your mind until it becomes like an elastic band. The band never goes back to its original size, it always grows along with your understanding. It's the difference between calculated risk and made up fears.

This elastic band analogy counts for everything. I was uncomfortable publishing my first ever blog post - having my thoughts and opinions out there for everyone to see and pick apart. Now I don't even flinch at writing a blog. Now I'm writing a book.

The first time I went to live by myself in Thailand, it was a big deal with all the things needing to be in place and the mental capacity to see it through. Talking about these things and doing them are completely different. But now, after several trips away I wouldn't think twice about booking a flight, organising a visa and everything else involved with a move overseas, meeting people, making friends, going on day and overnight trips, singing in a bar with locals. I'd just go and do it.

"Starting a company is like throwing yourself off the cliff and assembling an airplane on the way down."
- Reid Hoffman

Redefine what a risk is and start taking more of them. I promise at the other side is whatever you want, as long as you have the persistence and desire to see it through.

You're going to have problems and setbacks, but you might as well get on with it and start finding out what they are as you approach them. Putting it off stops you realising your thoughts aren't real concerns and that these hypotheticals stop you finding the real risks in order to get where you want to be.

Don't be afraid of failure and start making mistakes today. You'll learn from them and they'll get less frequent. Ignore the *'what if's'* and stop worrying about what people will say. The ones that will think negatively and poke fun at your failures are always the ones who are never even in the game.

People will give you excuses all day for why they aren't doing something. You tell them it's just an excuse, then and they say:

"Pffft, you don't understand"

No, I understand all right, I just haven't been telling myself what you've been telling yourself long enough to build this giant wall of bullshit to scare you. The longer you dwell on something and refuse to take action the bigger the fictitious problem becomes in your head, until it's so big that it seems insurmountable. It takes someone to see it from the outside and say *"What are you talking about? That's easy to fix, here's exactly how!"* or *"In my experience what you're describing has literally never happened."*

People say:

"Why should I start this business? So and so already has a huge market share."

"There are already big companies in my city doing that!"

Do people say they're not going to become a surgeon because they live in the top place in the world for surgeons? It never happens, so why do we do it for business? All it proves is there's a market, and if you're business is a good one (which is what you should be aiming for anyway, regardless of the competition) you'll get a slice. Then it's about getting better and winning more business because **you're** getting better. You never need to overtake the market leader, but you definitely won't if you never even start.

There are ways around everything, no excuses. You're just not willing to do it, to sacrifice, to hold yourself accountable.

You'll never be short of *'generics'* wanting to give you their two-bit advice:

- You don't want to do it that way!
- Have you thought about this?
- You should do it this way!
- What if this happens?
- You don't want to buy **that** car!
- In this economy?
- Surely you don't want to do your motorcycle test in winter?!
- What about your credit rating?
- You're not going to Thailand yourself, are you?!
- What about your savings?
- You don't want to…

OK, why don't I just sit in a dark room with a thumb up my ass and hide from consequences. Do those that spout that drivel ever end up doing anything of note aside from reluctantly fucking the partner they settled for, having kids they resent and clocking in some bullshit 9 to 5 job?

Healthy skepticism or weighing up pros and cons is fine, but most of the time these types of people are just being horrendous, dream killing, pussies!

Your excuses are bullshit and they are holding you back.

How long have you been acting like this? What could you have achieved had you taken the risks that are quite frankly minuscule in relation to your safety, but you build up into some bullshit nonsense? Every fucking person thinks their excuses are unique.

They're not and they're bullshit. Stop it. Today. Right now, stop with the excuses.

Are you willing to go against your friends, family, teachers, boss, whoever? Are you willing to eat noodles every night? Are you willing to sleep in your car and shower at the gym?

Generic people don't take risks. Generic people live generic lives - and you must decide if you're OK with generic or not.

If you're not taking risks, you're not living. You're choosing short term comfort over an outcome in your head that'll probably never even happen!

13

PLAUDITS

I noticed something on Facebook the other day. A woman in one of the marketing groups I'm a member of was posting about how getting a new job or achieving a promotion in an existing job gets a ton of likes, but something entrepreneurial like starting a business gets very little comparative response.

If you're thinking is in line with this, then I'm going to stop you there:

People do not give a shit.

Your friends, family, loved ones …everyone in your life gives a shit about you in some capacity, in varying degrees. In this instance I'm not talking about not being supportive or discouraging you or saying *"good for you"*. You'll get that, or at least you should if they're worth a damn.

I'm talking about the level of plaudits you're looking for, the kind that the woman was talking about, because they're not there. I repeat:

If you're doing this for plaudits, then do not even start.

People have their own lives, their own goals, their own problems. They don't exist to prop up your ego, to tell you every day that what you're doing is *"oh-so-amazing"*. They exist to focus on their own life, and there's nothing wrong with that.

Being an entrepreneur isn't typically relatable to anyone other than **other entrepreneurs**. You can't expect to post something like *"Handed in my notice"*, *"Starting my own business"* and receive as many likes (or whatever the ego-stroke is) as someone talking about a new job or promotion. People can't put themselves in those shoes as easily. It's not as relatable.

OK, so that covers the people that **do** actually care about you. Do you seriously expect the guy that you went to high school with, who wrestles with his poorly paid job every day to put food on the table for his kids, who takes heat from his nagging wife as soon as he gets home to log in to Facebook on his downtime and see you posting a jaunt down *"how cool am I"* lane?

Again, people don't like you achieving anything that points out flaws they have or things they don't have. While new jobs and promotions are great - they're safe and achievable in relation to the employed life of a person who's reading it.

If you're doing this because you need plaudits, then don't do it. To show people you can do it, well that's another thing, but don't expect them to throw a party for your big reveal.

Being an entrepreneur is a lonely road, no matter how many people you surround yourself with. You cannot expect plaudits before you are established and actually achieving something. They **will** give a shit once they see you buying nice houses or cool cars or tropical holidays or designer clothes or shiny jewellery or fancy dinners - generally splashing cash, because that's what most see as a benchmark for success.

People in your life won't get it until you're making money. That'll be their benchmark. They look at you oddly when you say that money doesn't validate you and you don't need it to buy a bunch of *'stuff'*. They probably won't believe you at first, then disbelief moves into resentment that you haven't taken **their path**, then they have to justify to themselves why they took their path and not yours.

People will try to poke holes in your lifestyle, deliberately navigating around the obvious benefits. They'll grasp at anything to vindicate the opposing lifestyle choice they've taken.

I hear it all the time. I was at a birthday party a few years ago with a bunch of young, pretentious douchebags, all talking about what they earn, what their mortgages looked like, how their investment portfolio is doing, wives giving sly digs about their husbands, husbands making passive aggressive comments showing they clearly resent their kids…

The conversation turns to me:

"What do you do"

I run a business.

"Oh cool, what do you do?"

Digital Marketing & Business Growth.

"You must make a lot of money then?!"
(Not paraphrasing, that was the exact line)

Nah, I'm more interested in time than money and giving value by helping people. I do around 15 hours of actual work a week while travelling.

"Yeah, but you could make a load more money if you worked harder, yeah?"
(Not kidding, exact quote again)

Why do we need validation in the form of earnings? So that you can point at a number and say:

"In my head this is what I'm worth and I'm trying to assess if my number is higher than yours to see where I fit-in socially compared to you."

It's fucking boring.

However, most of the entrepreneurs I know aren't wired that way. If you have no interest in splashing cash on fancy consumer goods or *'how big is my dick'* houses then most people won't see the correlation between what you have and your success, so you'll never get the plaudits.

Why do you want the plaudits? Maybe you took a lot of shit in school, maybe your parents never encouraged you, maybe your teacher told you you'd never amount to anything or maybe you came from nothing. It doesn't matter – do it for yourself and your own satisfaction.

Those kinds of plaudits are a waste of time anyway. Ignore those who put the highest value on *'stuff'*. Realise that time, experience and the quality of your day to day life are more important than money and trinkets.

We're more side-tracked into buying consumer garbage than ever. I'm not saying don't buy the things you want, but if you want them, do it for yourself, not other people.

You cannot create the life you want for yourself based around other people's perception of happiness and wealth.

Support is a different thing. I've got many business owning friends who help support my goals, who I bounce ideas off, who I generally go for a beer and shoot the shit with. I've got great family and great friends, but I don't expect them to give me a pat on the back. I pat myself on the back whenever I think it's genuinely deserved.

Talking about business and entrepreneurship doesn't always work with those in employment. You won't get the mindset or the feedback that's relevant to what you're trying to achieve. Those listening will sometimes unwittingly skew your thinking, or even completely warp it into something unrecognisable. You must be stronger than that and block out all the noise.

The better I do, the more different I become, and my circle gets smaller – but in a good way. It's important to be comfortable in your own skin, find your own hobbies, enjoy your own company and surround yourself with a circle that truly matters.

WHAT MATTERS

Reprogram the standard, typical, social construct:

- Have a house by age…
- Be married by age…
- Have kids by age…
- Have pensions and 401k's.
- Drive certain cars.
- Buy certain clothes.
- Eat in certain places.
- Wear certain jewellery.

How amazing is it to have that hot tub in your back garden …you know …that hot tub you never use …unless your bragging to your friend or trying to make the neighbours jealous?

If you have a job: Is it making you happy or keeping you distracted?

If you have a partner: Are they making you happy or keeping you distracted?

Your toys: Are they making you happy or keeping you distracted?

If you have interest rates and a mortgage: Are they making you happy or keeping you distracted?

Ask yourself:

"Am I doing this because it makes me happy or am I putting up with it to keep me distracted from how my life isn't where I want it to be, or the unknown alternative?"

What does success mean to you? When you hear the word success, what do you picture in your head? For most, it means money…

Maybe a sportsperson on a podium or lifting a trophy. Delving deeper? It looks like big houses, nice cars, fancy clothes, jewellery, exotic holidays, champagne, fancy food and lavish gifts. Where did we learn this? Because it **is** taught. From the media to pressure from parents and peers. It defines and cripples people, keeps them perpetually dissatisfied, and mentally unwell.

When you make it about the houses, cars, clothes, jewellery ...it never ends. Ever.

There's always the next thing. You think:

"If I can just get that kind of house, own that car, have that watch…"

"…that partner, that husband or wife…"

…you always want more.

I'm already successful. I wanted to be financially free, to live and earn on my own terms and work the hours that I wanted to work. To be at peace in my head and to understand what life means to me.

I'm here already.

Success is when you stop wanting more.

Don't misunderstand, this isn't a call to be proud of average, to be proud of not earning enough, being on the breadline, unable to support yourself or your family. Or some unhealthy notion about money that every person who has it in abundance somehow attained it unethically like Lex Luther or Montgomery Burns, but success **is** when you're happy in yourself and your situation.

Keep putting more cherries on top of that sundae, I encourage it. You can have as many of those cherries as you want, they can drown the sundae for all I care; but the sundae itself is the success and the most important part of your life.

Success doesn't have to be a smug grin, strutting around, putting a key in your Ferrari and driving to your mansion. Redefine what it means to you personally and refuse pressure from the outside world telling you what it is.

People can be so vapid:

"I want to be a millionaire"

Why? What does that mean? You want to say *"suck it"* to your enemies? You want to rock up in a Bentley to your family Christmas party? You think that'll make you happy? That constant needy stream of validation?

It's the same as consumerism. If you are constantly buying things for short term satisfaction and validation then you are always wanting the next thing - the bigger thing, you'll eventually burn out and realise you were chasing a mirage. You need to get happy in your head - do what you enjoy to win at life.

You do you, and if it ends up *'too late'* then that's the way you rolled. Don't sweat shit so much. It's only life. The chance of you being here is so minute – throw caution to the wind and act like it!

Find out what is important to you, and don't be swayed by social norms. My dad functions easily on 6 hours sleep per night - I typically sleep 8 or 9. Entrepreneurial books would say that's 14 hours a week I'm losing to productivity. The effect on my body if I was getting 14 hours less sleep per week, every single week of my life would be terrible. That's 728 hours less sleep per year! I don't want to think about how that impacts my mental and physical health, given I know how much better I feel just with those 2 extra hours per night.

Consuming makes us unhappy. We're absolutely spoiled in this day and age with what we have, yet we're completely dissatisfied most of the time and wanting more. Like a drug that keeps us addicted it never actually solves anything. Stop buying and consuming shit that you don't need.

> *"We are what we do, and if you just make money - you become money."*
> - Ray Arcel, Hands of Stone

I've tried, miserably, most of my life, to be cool and relevant. Ever since school I've tried desperately hard to fit in. It never worked and now I know why. Fitting in is really hard to do, we're all unique. Not necessarily amazing, but unique none the less. We break our fucking backs to fit in, it's perverse.

Those that manage to achieve fitting in will do everything in their power to keep you in your box, stop you spreading your wings, mock your every achievement if that achievement isn't something traditionally *'cool'*.

Fuck them and fuck their shitty drone system that exists to keep you down and make you hesitate to have fun away from the usual *'stuff'*. I was afraid to escape trying to fit in, what it would mean, how I would be mocked, provoked, how I wouldn't measure up, and I feared failure.

Now? Fitting in is my biggest fear

I see the facade for what it is. Consumer garbage, work, being sensible …how fucking boring.

Most only realise it once it's too late. They've committed themselves in all manner of ways that stifles future growth and excitement. We're sold being sensible and overthinking everything.

We're supposed to:

- Get educated.
- Work in a box.
- Save.
- Get a mortgage.
- Start a family.
- Watch TV.
- Be thankful if we're able to *'fit in'* a hobby or a passion project.

Just about everyone does it. I'm sure it's for some people but not the whole fucking species. I escaped that hamster wheel but it's always there, trying to suck me back in.

Never fully grow up – maintain your child-like curiosity. All the people I know that are properly indoctrinated into *'adulting properly'* before their time are the most boring, unimaginative and dead inside people you'll ever have the misfortune of inviting into your soul.

Don't let anyone steal that fire.

The media force feeds us expectations of what everything should look like. Drones, watching other drones. No connection. Although, with social media we're more connected than ever, despite which - it has given the drones a bigger voice. Making it even harder to listen to the voice in your ear, your head, your heart; instead of some douchebag with a shitty opinion on a screen.

The need to consume has made us soft and selfish. He needs that car, she wants a wedding - not a marriage. Worse than ever, even worse than in the 80's when greed was good, it defines you now, it's what you look for in a person - a token on your arm like a fucking accessory. Loyalty is shattered in place of entitlement.

What makes us put up with stuff we're unhappy with? What makes us grumble about it then go right back into putting up with it? People say

"Oh, it's alright for you!"

Don't they think I had a million excuses I could've used? Truly ask yourself if your reasoning is genuine ...or just an excuse to keep you in your comfort zone.

The weather, the country, a job, a relationship? Who do we blame? Someone else? Where you were born through accident of birth? The government? What are you putting up with that you should change and make your life better?

Don't just threaten to do it either – make it happen!

I hear excuses constantly. Then people get really offended when you call them out on it.

"How dare you say I should be able to do it, despite taking care of my kids!"

No, how dare **you** use your kids as leverage in a conversation to excuse your inaction! You think people don't build successful businesses side hustling while working 2 jobs and taking care of their kids? I work with those people every day!

You don't want success badly enough to work 1 hour at night on your dream instead of sleeping, instead of your YouTube and Netflix escapism. You want to do the mental masturbation, you want to sit and fantasise about scenarios and do the fun stuff around the outside of your dream and none of the learning you need to do to get where you need to be.

After you've heard the excuses a thousand times from people who just cannot be honest with themselves for one second, stare their ego in the face and say:

"I don't want it badly enough, yet. I need to get to that place first. Everything else is an excuse."

it gets utterly mind numbingly tedious - yet I'm expected to politely nod my head because calling you out on it is considered rude or impolite.

How about you read a book on personal development and find out why you lie to protect yourself. While you're at it, buy the business book - because you claim to know nothing about that. Then buy the marketing book - because you know nothing about that. Hell, buy a book or do a Google search for any part of anything that you don't understand. Then seek out a mentor or a coach who will kick your ass and refuse to tolerate your excuses until you do it.

Alternatively, hide in your excuses and *'what ifs'*.

Entrepreneurs are not born. Every single thing you don't know was overcome by someone who was willing to work it out. Come to me when you're ready to work, not make excuses:

"I would be travelling the world like you if I didn't have my kids."

"I would be running my own business like you if I didn't have my kids."

No you fucking wouldn't. You wouldn't because of **you**. Start owning that and move on. You're using your kids as a shield to protect your own ego - tell someone else who wants to listen to that because I won't tolerate it.

Tell those other people and watch them pat you on the head while they tell you that you're right and that it sucks, because there's only so long that will last before those people get fed up with your excuses. They don't care why, and they can see the truth – they just won't tell you.

Everyone has the same opportunity:

"He got it because he is a trust fund baby!"

"She got it because she's hot and guys throw money at that!"

"I never had a stable upbringing or a safety net."

Forget everyone else. In the western world everyone has the same opportunity to come from absolutely nothing. Your excuses are just that. People let life happen to them. They **think** life is what happens to you.

Life is what you go out and do - very few exceptions. Stop doing what everyone else is doing.

As I say, I work with people every day that have these excuses. Only these people never turned them into excuses. They never allowed them to be excuses or for those excuses to define them as a person, make them a victim or stop what they wanted to achieve.

What I've learned most in the recent past is:

Wherever you go, there you are.

I always strived for that little bit more cash (even though money has never really motivated me), to live in a certain place, to have a specific relationship.

Nothing is more important than sorting your head out, otherwise the pursuit of happiness is a fool's errand. It doesn't exist without the state of mind.

I've had the money, the tropical beach and the perfect couple scenarios and none of it is fulfilling without looking internally.

Stop chasing whatever it is and start building peace and understanding in your own head.

Don't be fooled by supercars, mansions, watches. There's only learning and action. Learn and take action. You could be doing what I'm doing in no time, that's not a false dream. It takes time to build up to flash cars and houses if that's what you really want. But earning a living, staying somewhere nice? That's not a dream at all.

I retrained myself in around a month, eventually started winning clients and constantly improved my skills and services. I have the most bang average academic intelligence, but I applied myself to something and didn't stop until I reached my goals.

CONSUMERISM

We're absolutely spoiled in this day and age with what we have, yet we're completely dissatisfied most of the time, always wanting more.

When we buy something we get an endorphin spike, which doubles up if it's an online order, because when it arrives we get another spike. How long does that last? Not worth the price of the product anyway.

But we keep doing it. We set goals for trinkets, for houses we overstretch on, for clothes that are in fashion and we sacrifice our most valuable asset – **time**, for the privilege.

> *"We buy things we don't need, with money we don't have, to impress people we don't like."*
> - Tyler Durden, Fight Club

Stop buying and consuming shit you don't need.

Consuming makes us unhappy.

So, what does that mean? It means consumerism isn't the answer. I'm not saying don't buy the things you want - but ask yourself why you're buying them. Is it because you really want the thing, for you, personally? Or is it to keep up appearances? To make people jealous or envy you?

Our entire social framework is geared around consuming *'stuff'*. If you're a heavy consumer now, as most people are, you're probably thinking about the level you need to get at that's *"just out of reach, but when I get there I'll be so happy and relaxed"*. Understand that you never get there. Every time you reach that goal it gets replaced with a bigger goal. You don't even know you're doing it.

People survive on goals, hope and purpose.

Let's say, hypothetically, you have everything you ever wanted. You and your family are incredibly healthy, you have an obscene amount of cash ensuring you survive in luxury the rest of your days, you have the house you want, the cars you love to drive and you generally have the best of everything.

Anyone who's made it to that point throughout history who has spoken frankly about it has said it's not what you think it is. It's not enough. We're not wired for *'things'* to be the finish line.

The secret is that there's no finish line. Just more goals and the hope of achieving them.

If you have all the things above outlined, then maybe you want to travel the world. Maybe you want to set up a foundation to help the less fortunate. These are goals, with hope and purpose.

You're never going to stop feeling that feeling. Don't chase the consumer garbage. Set goals, and when you hit them - set some more. Accept that there is no finish line and that life is just goals, hope and purpose. No goals mean no meaning. No meaning means either wasting away or dying.

The more you succeed and the more you make your dreams reality, the humbler you become. You realise what a waste of time consumerism is, you realise what a waste of time living on social media is. Even though you've achieved what you've always wanted you feel less inclined to brag than you ever did before.

Some people around you will feel like they need to test your belief, like you're putting on an act. They'll make cheap comments, digs, sarcasm. Anything as open as an insult down to a throwaway line as if to give you *'the reality check you need'* - usually in the form of a fear they've always had for not stepping into the arena.

The more the people in your life go down the traditional, social norm routes getting more dissatisfied, the deeper they get and the more they take it out on you with their shitty comments.

When you're a business owner it's not enough to have your own self-doubt – you need to deal with everyone else's doubts about you, too.

The world is full of boring people, so don't be another one. Do not listen to other people. Never pay attention to people's words, only their actions. When you do this, you'll start to see the inconsistency in both. Only take advice or critique from other people in the game ...and those people won't be the type to give cheap digs or discourage you in the first place.

People who are the least remarkable are the most pass remarkable.

Also understand that despite what I'm saying, you are not above criticism – do not surround yourself with sycophants. The point is, if someone's giving constructive criticism - just make sure they're worth a damn before you let it penetrate into your logic, never mind your soul.

As a consumer you are reactive. As a producer you are proactive. Producers manipulate and sell their products based on your primal feelings such as: Fear, laziness, superiority, snobbery, approval and ego. Do you want to be sold to? Or do you want to do the selling?

OK, so we can't *win* because we always want more. What's the solution?

Don't be in the game.

The million-dollar secret is: Be a producer, not a consumer. A producer is someone that creates things for other people to buy. That might be a physical thing, it might be a service, but the wealthy are as such because they produce things for people to buy - consumers are those that do nothing other than pay for those things.

Producers count on it.

Become a producer and get the freedom, because time is the most important thing you have. Consumers do not have time like producers do.

At time of writing - my car and motorbike combined aren't worth 3k, even though they are big parts of my hobbies. My mortgage is half what the bank were willing to lend me, so I have comfortability and the flexibility to travel.

This is not a brag, this is explaining how it works and how being a consumer is a sacrifice. Not being a blind consumer, investing back in your business, being minimalist and willing to do whatever it takes like I mentioned - sleeping in your car and showering at your gym is how you do something of substance and character.

Shallow desires don't inspire action - being willing to make sacrifices does.

Produce and give yourself the freedom and the money to do whatever you want with your time. Time with family, friends, your loved ones and on your own. Not restricted by someone else telling you what you can and can't do.

I'll focus on posting encouragement, knowledge, building people up, designing systems that help people grow and hopefully learn something that motivates them – I'll let others post on social media about how the US president spelled a word wrong on twitter, or why Angelina Jolie and Brad Pitt split, or why your political party should've won the election.

Don't be distracted. Be a producer, not a consumer.

VICTIMHOOD & ACCOUNTABILITY

People are insufferably whiney, perpetual victims. I've especially seen an insurgence of it in the last few years. Everything is someone else's fault. We have very little accountability any more.

Most of your problems are your own. People can't handle this, but it's true. If you trace it back to the source it's usually a bad decision, or a lazy one. Take problems in your life that you dwell on, trace it right back to the very source, to the beginning and be honest with yourself. Most of the time it could've been prevented or changed with you taking action, but you never did.

Giving something else the blame is the easy way out. It tricks your mind into telling you that you're the victim. You're not a victim, you just make bad choices like every other human. How you excel is in owning them. It's one of the hardest things to do, but if you can master this you'll move forward at an exponential rate.

Granted, sometimes it **is** the cards you're dealt and everything about your character is how you stand up and trade blows with it until it doesn't own or define you. Don't dwell on it until it eats all of your soul.

Nothing is important other than realising nothing is important. In the grand scheme of everything, of time, importance and significance, everything you do, good or bad, is but a speck of dust in a giant cosmos.

Don't sweat shit so much!

When you're a victim you act out and put that mentality into the world.

I have a client who worked hard to build up a successful small business. He has a bunch of boomers posting shit like: *"All right for those that can afford it!"* on his Facebook adverts, which is not uncommon on many of my clients ads.

28

Now, my client:

- Worked hard for years to build a business from nothing.
- Employs a few people.
- Additionally, trains himself in his own time.
- Reinvests a little profit into advertising to get more business.
- Employs more people as his business grows.

All to have these utter ambulance chasers ruin his paid advert with their shitty, cry-baby, perpetual victim comments.

The advert was about how his business transformed another woman's life, the kind of result you couldn't put a price on!

I've even had hate on an advert I created on behalf of a charity whose sole purpose is to train underprivileged kids a new skill and then help them find a job with that skill! This is further proof that you'll get haters no matter what you do. So, the fear of failure and what others think is a pointless exercise.

Victimhood manifests itself particularly on the subject of politics in social media chatter:

"I voted for _____ and if you didn't then you're an idiot! Don't reply to my post because I'll delete you!!"

Do you know how to better the life of yourself and those worse off around you? Do it yourself. Trump, Clinton, May, Corbyn or any other politician (regardless of how many times you digitally suck them off) aren't going to do it for you.

"If voting made a difference, they wouldn't let us do it."
- Mark Twain

…because…

"The best argument against democracy is a five-minute conversation with the average voter."
- Winston Churchill

If you tick a box and expect someone to change your life for you - I've got some bad news. If your waiting for a politician to change your life or the lives of those around you, you clearly haven't been paying attention for the decades you've been on this earth.

Your choice of mind control in the 21st century is your ability to surround your social media following only with others that have the beliefs that you currently hold and the dogmas you subscribe to.

Social media has been hijacked by miserable fucks who hate their life. It always seems to be the ones that could write what they know about life on the back of a stamp with a marker that shout the loudest. When people repeatedly comment negatively or complain on social media it's because they're unfulfilled in life or have issues they're unwilling to solve.

Don't be that person. Own your mistakes, your failings and your shortcomings. As soon as you do, you can start addressing them. Who are you hiding them from anyway?

The only person you need to be competing against is the person you were yesterday.

I've heard consultants, coaches and mentors say their clients regularly complain along the lines of:

"I could've done that. I already knew that. I didn't need to pay you to tell me that!"

But you didn't and **that's the point!** You don't take action. Something being said to you in the simplest possible way, getting it out of your head and into words or onto paper with a plan and accountability is sometimes what it takes to actually get you where you want to be.

I'm good at holding myself accountable with the big picture but my day to day has me struggling. That's why I pay someone to check in and make sure I'm following through with all my targets and goals.

I admitted to myself the problems I had in my working life. I couldn't fix them by myself, so I paid to have it done just like anything else that I can't do myself. Just because I can't fix my own car doesn't mean I drive around with a problem getting progressively worse until the car finally blows up - I pay to get it fixed.

Your life, your mental health, your business – whatever it is, take action and get it fixed! Otherwise you'll procrastinate, the problem will get bigger in your head and you'll carry it around with you every day, you won't improve, and you'll probably post utter shit on Facebook.

Nobody wants that.

If someone's holding you accountable and pushing you on in your business, then your business will make much more additionally than what you pay the consultant, mentor or coach. This should be the same with any service you pay for to enhance your business.

Studies show accountability in any discipline is almost essential, because it's easy to bullshit yourself, but impossible when you have someone holding you accountable.

Don't be stubborn. Be willing to spin on a dime. Don't double down on something when you realise it's wrong because it's easier to keep going and hope for the best that it works out.

If we're talking about an opinion or a process in your business or anything else - be brave and be willing to stop. Hold your hands up, don't try to style it out. People go on for years persisting with the same mindset or process, and will defend it, knowing it's wrong instead of facing it head on. Lying to yourself feels shitty but once you start owning things and being honest with yourself and other people, it's amazing.

You got something wrong - so what? Do people not get things wrong? It's like any dogma you're taught from a young age - you've believed it for so long that it's easier to keep going with it rather than all the doubts you have in the back of your head. The feeling in your gut and in the back of your mind is telling you that it's wrong. Face it, own it and be free of your mistakes or your beliefs. Grow.

FREEDOM

I retired at 27. Eight years ago when I started my business.

That's what it feels like. Not that I want to take up golf, or lunch with the ladies, but after you've worked *"real"* jobs for years you get an appreciation for the freedom. You get to do what you want to do, with no one to answer to.

I feel like I'm unemployed. I don't have any of that dread for work. Waking up every day is a question of:

"What's in store today?"

...not...

"How can I get through this as quickly, quietly and least painfully as possible?"

Yeah, I have stress but nothing like that feeling of hearing my alarm buzz every work day and wishing my life away for some respite on the other side, trading 5 days of servitude for 2 days of freedom.

Fuck that. Never again.

I was broke, but I felt like I got a raise! When I quit my job, I went from earning a good salary and commission for years, right down to zero. I get asked a lot, mostly from clients, or when I do interviews about what the number one piece of advice I can give is. It's not so much advice as a statement:

Time is more important than money

This is the most important thing you will read in this book.

Stop trading your time for money. I'd love to show that scared guy 8 years ago what things look like now. I traded hating 5 days a week to never hating another day again. How can I argue with that?

"The price of anything is the amount of life you exchange for it."
- Henry David Thoreau

Social media used to be fun. Now everyone uses it as a support mechanism to vent their shit and impose their ignorant beliefs on their equally miserable friends. The reason is:

Escapism.

It's the same reason why we watch Netflix (although I love a good series binge myself), the reason we play video games and the reason people get excited when Kanye West says something ridiculous on Twitter.

It's respite from the hard day. Days are hard in entrepreneurship too, but the business becomes your passion, your belief, your drive, your purpose, your baby – whatever. You're not hiding from it until the next time you need to roll your sleeves up to get in there again. It's something you want to improve. Something you created from nothing that grows as a result of your effort.

When you don't hate what you do, you don't need to retire. Retirement funds as we know them now were primarily introduced around the 1960's **in case** people outlived their life expectancy. It wasn't something to work towards in order to sit and do nothing!

Studies show that in retirement many of us fast track our deaths due to lack of sufficient stimulation. Our brain needs regular exercise, the kind it got used to from working, solving problems and balancing a family and social life.

When we retire, the lack of stimulation slows us down until we stop.

Do something you love for a living. Instead of spending all of your money on a nest egg, spend time on a skill you can get so prolific at that you then adopt in retirement around ways to make you money.

You might die before you retire, and your payments were for nothing. You might get to the retirement age and the government's sold it out from under you.

Don't rely on a system. The system is rigged to fail you. Rely on yourself to be self-sufficient! Keep your mind active in retirement by maintaining work and setting new challenges. If you never retire, then it's never *'the beginning of the end'*.

Find something you'll enjoy doing as work and take that into retirement. Start a business in retirement, it doesn't have to cost money to start up, it could even be consulting of some kind.

Ideally, if you're not at retirement age yet, start your business now and don't wish your life away for a date that's years in the future so you can sit and watch daytime TV.

"I don't really see a need to retire as long as I am having fun."
\- Stan Lee

EDUCATION

My feelings on education itself will come in the Business section. For now, let's look at it from the Mindset point of view.

As I said in the intro – a solid early education is essential but beyond that, the most important things to learn are what **you** want to learn.

> *"Formal education will make you a living, self-education will make you a fortune."*
> - Jim Rohn.

I had to read everything that I now know. All the personal development came from reading first, then *'acting out'* the steps - there were no magical epiphanies.

Discomfort and putting yourself out there is where the growth is. I would not have understood that unless I read it. I would've attributed it to luck every time I achieved something through discomfort.

I had to read that and understand cause and effect. Learn things. If you're unsure - act out what you've read and see what happens. Don't do the same shit and wonder why you're getting the same results you always have.

Learn from people who have done it. Look at someone you admire and read their book. Learn from them, their mistakes and what they did to triumph – then replicate it. There is no reason that you can't.

They are not special. They are made of the same matter as you. No excuses.

What's sad is the pressure from parents. They doom their kids to the same shit sandwich they were served up. Forcing them to go through the same process as they had, even though they hate their life. If you have these parents, or anyone else in your life that's acting similar, talking in your ear, then you must quiet that noise and blaze your own trail. There is no honour in living your life to suit someone else.

If it turns out to be the wrong decision, then so be it. You made your choice, but the choice **was yours**. At least you went for it, and no matter how badly you fail – no-one can take that away from you. You looked in the mirror and said:

"This is who I am, this is what I want to pursue, this is the subject I will self-study at, this is who I want to learn from, this is my plan, and this is how I see it playing out. If it doesn't go as smoothly as that then I'll make it work. If it doesn't work, then I took a shot – how many people can say they're taking that shot? Who are they to judge anything?!"

So, start learning and start taking action. You **must** take action. The more you do, the more you learn and the more you achieve. Do not get stuck in the comfort zone of hiding away, reading and planning – nothing happens without execution. No matter how much you read it won't mean a thing unless you take action. The action makes you learn ten times quicker than any amount of reading ever will.

Don't sacrifice years of hard work and the lifetime cost of a degree to be just as miserable as you would be in a poorly paid 9 to 5 with the only difference being - more money. Defy the education system, defy the rat race, defy working for the man. Choose your own education and go it alone. Get more prolific at your craft, learn from your mistakes, refine your processes, become a better businessperson. Educate yourself in every aspect of it and **grow**.

BELIEF

When I talk about growth I mean, as time goes on, you begin what I call *'stacking belief'* and that growth becomes exponential. Let me explain...

Stepping out of your comfort zone is the worst feeling. I've never gotten used to it, in fact the anxiety gets worse as I get older and more set in my ways. But I know at the other side of that feeling is being able to **own** the thing that once made me uncomfortable and then take in my stride. Then from taking it in my stride to not even thinking about it, to the point where it's normalised.

- It was hard writing this first ever book and putting it out there.
- If I write another book it'll be quite hard but a damn sight easier.
- The one after that will be normalised.
- The one after that will be *"I should probably write a book on that"* and it'll just happen, I'll just go ahead and write it.

On the other side of any process or activity, no matter how nervous it makes you, once it's repeated often enough it becomes normalised and the mindset becomes *"I can't believe I was ever stressed about that"*. You **must** understand this at the point of doing something for the first time. Don't let doubt control what you do and what you want to become.

Use adversity, discomfort, anxiety and fear as a way to grow. I started learning Direct Response Copywriting around 2 years ago. After researching the subject tirelessly (I read 6 books before I started implementing it) I knew it was the way to go.

In my industry, copy written by a marketing agency is very *'pizazz'*. It looks great and it's written better than the client could typically write it themselves. If it's done correctly with a modicum of marketing competence it will explain the product well and have the right calls to action in the right places.

Much like most marketing agencies would have their team do - I'd been doing this for years to agreeable nods from my clients' every time…

…but it doesn't get results the way Direct Response Copywriting does.

I **knew** if I took my clients in this direction they would go from *'typically good results'* to *"my books are full!"* results.

Pretty soon after I started implementing the strategy and receiving some mentoring from experts in Direct Response Copywriting, who would look over my own copy and improve my efforts further – my clients were almost immediately seeing results, much better than the traditional marketing speak.

Around the same time, I won a new client (on a very respectable retainer) to do their marketing. I immediately skipped the pizazz and went for the Direct Response approach.

It took a long time to write the pages. I had to actually think about what I was writing, rather than the tidy *'marketing-speak'* which I now had on autopilot thanks to years of my own conditioning. I had to ask the client lots of questions every week, learning the right angle and selling point (more on this in the Marketing section).

But:

The client didn't like it.

It took me so much longer to do and it wasn't factual, rigid like the typical *"Here's what it is, buy it if you want"*. It flowed, it focused more on the emotions of the reader, it explained why they shouldn't be without the service, it created fear, scarcity and took them on a journey, it told stories to make the reader feel relatable, it humanised my client …but they didn't want it.

In fact, they asked for a refund.

Something I'd never experienced before. They didn't like the change in their copy, even though I knew it would benefit them in the long run - even though I had examples of how it totally changed other existing client's results.

- I could have begged them to stay on (not my style).
- I could've offered to change the copy to something more generic.
- I could've repeatedly reasoned about how it would create the growth they were looking for.

…but I knew I would be selling out what I believed, so I refunded them. I stood my ground and explained why, but I wasn't going to chase a company that didn't believe from the start in what I was trying to do.

We parted ways.

I don't know a bigger test of belief than that.

Always be willing to walk away. You start your own business to be free and to relieve yourself of the burdens of employment:

- Being commanded to do things.
- Being told when you'll do them.
- To work more than you're willing to work.
- To take any form of abuse, manipulation or false blame.

No amount of money is worth your integrity or your mental health. Drop the client. It's never worth it.

Likely, the only thing stopping you from doing what you want to do is conformation that it will work beforehand. You want to protect yourself from failing or looking stupid. Unfortunately, it doesn't work that way. You have to take action until the belief becomes real. You have to act in the face of your fears, your doubt and your worry.

Once you get out of the trenches, failing sometimes and winning other times – the action teaches you that the odds are usually in your favour when you take massive action. It creates a loop where eventually:

- You **start** with real belief that the *'thing'* can be done.
- Which means you take more positive action. Action that isn't half hearted to protect yourself from failure and you make better decisions because your mind is in a better place.
- Which means you get better results …because of the greater action.
- Which gives you **more** belief that the next thing will work.
- You'll take even more action with the next thing.

…and so on, until all you're doing is stacking belief on top of more belief, taking greater action with a lesser fear of failure. You become unstoppable.

The most important thing to learn is - go for it. Things almost **never** work right away. You have to be willing to persist, take the shots and the knocks. You have to be able to live with the potential that other people will see you fail - but I swear to god it will come good for you if you persist. People treat success like it's an overnight thing.

It's amazing how many nights it takes to become an overnight success.

An overnight success is winning the lottery. Everything else is hard work. Do people honestly think a hit song was written on the Friday and number 1 in the music charts by Monday? It doesn't work like that. Even the shittest number 1 song involves time, dedication, persistence, sacrifice, understanding the market and a whole lot of self-belief.

It takes years learning instruments and writing words, understanding what works until you excel at it. It's handling rejection from the music industry until you get your *"lucky big break"* ...which is actually years of banging on the door.

Excuses like *"god given talent"* are used. People think when they say that - it's a compliment! It's an insult to hard work and dedication, honing your craft until there is no other way. Until you've **made** the way. Brute forced the way.

People don't want growth. They want to stand still while everything magically gets better around them.

Writing this reminded me of a blog post I wrote in 2016 about Conor McGregor:

Over the weekend, *"The Notorious"* Conor McGregor lost a fight *gasp*

If you've hopped on the UFC bandwagon recently, you might be confused into thinking this is new. Seasoned viewers will know it's not the first fight he's lost and there's no reason to suggest it will be the last.

In fact, McGregor has lost twice before – the latest has his professional record standing at 19-3. That's 19 wins and 3 losses (7-1 in the UFC).

Conor has legions of fans, but for every fan there's an armchair critic. People accuse him of being:

"Crass."
"Rude."
"Brash."
"Disrespectful."
"A show off."
"All talk."

They revel in his defeat.

A man that came from absolutely nothing, but through hard work, discipline, obsession to his craft and unwavering belief finds himself selling the biggest gates in UFC history, standing toe to toe and trading blows with a guy two weight classes above the Featherweight Title that McGregor currently holds.

The guy is an incredible role model for business owners. Here's why:

HARD WORK

"There's no talent here, this is hard work, this is an obsession. Talent does not exist. We are all equals as human beings. You could be anyone if you put in the time. You will reach the top, and that's that. I am not talented, I am obsessed."
- Conor McGregor

The above quote is very interesting. A number of years ago while watching a football documentary I discovered Zidane and the Brazilian Ronaldo weren't even the best players **in their school!** Two of the greatest players to have ever played the most popular sport in the world.

I always thought growing up that people were either born gifted or not. You had sportsmen, artists and quantum physicists in one corner, and you had 9 to 5'ers in the other. This is absolutely, fundamentally incorrect. You can apply yourself, dedicate yourself to any discipline, sport or otherwise and achieve anything you want.

Anything.

I mention this a lot during presentations – I was always average academically. Where I win is dedicating myself to my craft. If I'm not working, I'm reading up on how to do it better. Always looking to improve and learn. It's not a struggle because I enjoy it and see the rewards. Once you get those rewards it makes it easier to find the willingness to learn. It's not a chore or traditional *'working hard'* – it's enjoyable.

Need further proof? Michael Jordan was cut from the basketball team in sophomore year for simply **not being good enough.** MJ used the motivation to practice constantly until he **looked** like the most naturally gifted player in the history of the sport. Could you imagine what would have happened if he took the rejection like so many of us? What direction it would've taken his life?

He is one of the most decorated basketball players in history with a billion-dollar fortune.

HUSTLE

"I see fighters make funny videos about me and stick them on Facebook and get 20 likes. When I make a video, I sell it to Fox and make seven figures. That's the difference."
- Conor McGregor

This is part of the hard work above. You're a good fighter, you're getting better, your winning fights – how do you get noticed? McGregor is the absolute master of this. Marketing yourself is critical in any business. He is a great fighter but as anyone can see that's not how he's selling tickets and smashing pay per view records. **He's hustling.**

He's in everyone's face, he masters his message and projects it perfectly, he says what he means and he backs it up with his ability. If he's not stealing a title holder's belt off the table at a press conference, he's driving his new Rolls Royce Phantom droptop around LA, blasting Mariah Carey from its sound system!

What can you do differently to attract your clients or customers and how hard are you hustling to make it happen? Don't be afraid to be confident when you can back it up.

CONFIDENCE

"I'm not going to get somewhere and say, 'OK, I'm done.' Success is never final; I'll just keep on going. The same way as failure never being fatal. Just keep going. I'm going to the stars and then past them."
- Conor McGregor

Speaking of confidence, Conor McGregor has incredible self-belief. It's one of the hardest learned behaviours in life, never mind sport.

He was so confident about his previous fight that he knew exactly what was going to happen and told the press about it before the fight even took place! What happened? He knocked the guy out in 13 seconds, with one punch, in the exact manner as he said it would happen! His opponent was the only Featherweight Champion in UFC history. Why? He'd held it for 10 years since it was introduced!

If you provide a good product or service – have the conviction to talk about it and have faith that what you're doing is good. Even if you have a setback like McGregor's loss, don't let it dent your confidence. Dust yourself off and get back in the ring!

FEARLESSNESS

"I stormed in and put it all on the line. I took a shot and missed. I will never apologize for taking a shot. Shit happens. I'll take this loss like a man. I will not shy away from it. I will not change who I am. If another champion goes up 2 weights, let me know."
- Conor McGregor

To put his latest fight in context, Conor McGregor is currently the UFC Featherweight Champion. He was supposed to fight the current Lightweight Champion (the weight class above him) Rafael Dos Anjos, with the chance to become the first fighter in UFC history to hold two titles at the same time. Rafael pulled out with **less than two weeks' notice** and Nate Diaz was brought in, **a guy two weight classes above** Conor!

McGregor never flinched at the challenge and simply set about preparing for a different (and much heavier) opponent. As a result, despite hitting Nate with the kind of blows that would see someone in his own weight class fold like a cheap suit, Diaz could do enough to shrug them off and power on to the win.

He gets in the ring most often as well. He fought three times in 2015 and this one in early 2016. Most fighters have one or two fights per year.

What's Conor's attitude to a bigger challenge on short notice or a bump in the road in the form of a rare defeat? Let's go again!

Face your challenges head on, confront your fears and don't be afraid to lose or appear stupid.

SELF DICIPLINE

"I always teach myself calm and visualisation stuff. It's good to make your brain work more than your body."
- Conor McGregor

Conor works his ass off. His whole world is geared around either fighting, training for fighting or some sort of self-promotion. He's steeped his life in it and gets the rewards.

Unpopular with many, McGregor was actually on benefits in order to dedicate himself 100% to becoming a professional fighter and then on to becoming the champion in his weight class.

I'm not saying you should go on benefits, but what can you do to dedicate yourself for what you want to achieve? Obsessed is a word the weak use to describe the dedicated.

LOYALTY

"That's what I do this for, to secure my family's future. I don't care about anything else. I'm able to spoil people, and that's the best thing."
- Conor McGregor

Conor is famous for keeping those who were around from the start with him. He treats them well and reminds everyone regularly that his success is not just down to him, but a team effort thanks to all of them. He's now particularly generous to his long-suffering girlfriend who stood by him when he was doing low key fights, making sure his diet and training never wavered.

Last week I had a meeting with a potential client. It went extremely well as most of my meetings do. Having done my research beforehand so not to waste anyone's time and after listening to them tell me what they were looking for, I demonstrated why we would be a good fit and why I wanted them as a client.

They were very keen but shocked me in a way that left me extremely impressed. The owner went on to explain how they've tried to use all the same suppliers since the business first started out many years ago. As a result, they wanted to speak to their existing digital marketing provider to make sure they were OK with a change of direction or could they propose something different, rather than just hand everything over to me to take things to the next level.

I have the luxury of being able to pick and choose clients these days so I'm able to say I was so impressed by the attitude of this company, who favoured loyalty over blindly chasing the pound-sign potential of moving things over right away. Businesses could learn a thing or two with this type of loyalty and surrounding themselves with good people as Conor does.

HUMBLE IN DEFEAT

McGregor didn't throw his toys out of the pram. He congratulated his opponent and explained why they did a better job of approaching the fight than he did. He said:

"These things happen. I'll learn, I'll grow. I took a chance going up weight and it didn't work out. It is what it is, I'll face it like a man, like a champion and come back."
- Conor McGregor

We don't necessarily have opponents in business, but we often have competition and setbacks, problems and obstacles to overcome. How we deal with them is extremely important, though. The quote above encapsulates perfectly how we choose to deal with setbacks and our willingness to dust ourselves off and try again.

Like I said, despite all of this, it's easy to sit on the side lines and berate the guy. To haters of any kind I remind them of my favourite quote of all time:

"It is not the critic who counts; not the man who points out how the strong man stumbles, or where the doer of deeds could have done them better.

The credit belongs to the man who is actually in the arena, whose face is marred by dust and sweat and blood; who strives valiantly; who errs, who comes short again and again, because there is no effort without error and shortcoming; but who does actually strive to do the deeds; who knows great enthusiasms, the great devotions; who spends himself in a worthy cause;

Who at the best knows in the end the triumph of high achievement, and who at the worst, if he fails, at least fails while daring greatly, so that his place shall never be with those cold and timid souls who neither know victory nor defeat."
- Theodore Roosevelt

So, a few months after that article was written, Conor not only fought Nate Diaz again at the same weight class and avenged his loss – he went on to win another UFC title at a different weight class, making him the first person in UFC history to hold two belts simultaneously.

From there, he crossed disciplines and convinced boxer Floyd Mayweather Jr to compete in a multi-million-dollar superfight against him in 2017, quadrupling his net worth with one fight!

Start taking action and build the belief. Don't waste any more time. It took me until I was 20 to decide what I wanted to do, then it took 6 years of mental masturbation to actually follow through and make it a reality. Then 8 years of honing the business into the service it now provides and growing into the person I am today …and neither me nor the business will ever be the finished article.

If you haven't started yet, today would be a good time.

I also want to talk to you about *'Imposter Syndrome'*. If you feel like this, just a heads up - no matter how long you do what you do, no matter how good you get, no matter what landmarks you reach:

It never goes away.

Imposter Syndrome is just as it sounds, in that you feel like you're not good enough. Like you're some sort of fraud. Like it's all a dream and you're just waiting for the other shoe to drop despite all the facts on the contrary.

Where does it come from? Loads of reasons:

- Maybe you took a lot of shit in school.
- Maybe something good you achieved when you were younger got taken away from you.
- Maybe all of the things you've built up belief about in your life to this point was torn down by others.

It can be harder when your new business is a complete career change. You might not have any relevant qualifications, or you feel like you've got a lot less experience under you belt.

What's important is the **value** you deliver - nothing else. I will go into a lot more detail about value in the Business section later.

Whatever it is, it's a mirage. It's not real. It **feels** real - but it's bullshit. It doesn't help when it's combined with the Crab Bucket Mentality or general negativity of others.

You need to support yourself through it and find someone (or a few people) in your life you truly trust to help you combat the noise. Not just trusting enough not to shit all over whatever it is due to their own insecurities and inadequacies - but those that aren't sycophants who will tell you everything you do is amazing just for an easy life.

You need honest, objective opinions from those you respect - preferably those that are in (or have been) in a similar situation. Once you have these people in your life you must listen to them. You have to trust that they're being objective, otherwise you'll go round in circles saying:

"They're just saying it to be nice."

Remember, it doesn't matter how long you've been studying your chosen discipline, what school you went to, who you've worked for, what you've achieved - you're always still learning and you're never the finished article. You'd never want to be, or to get into a position where you think you are.

In fact, a further update on the Conor McGregor story – he reached the top and went off the rails. He took time off because he had a kid and to bask in the wealth and the fame for a while. He got into trouble, lost his next MMA fight, got in some more trouble because he stopped learning or trying to get better and chase his next goal as a fighter. He lost his identity, his purpose and has recently suffered dramatically for it.

Look at what others in your industry are producing. A look at the standard of others and what they charge can quickly build your confidence and let you know you're always on the right track. It's all about **value**. Are you providing value compared to the money your clients are spending with you? If you truly care, then you never need to worry about Imposter Syndrome.

People create roadblocks in their head – they simplify something down to *"It can't be done"*. It's indoctrinated into people.

They don't start out that way. Kids don't have it bred into them, which is why children take more risks and appear more free spirited.

Pushy parents, school and employment put them in a box that knocks it out of them.

Too many rules, too many invisible roadblocks, too much sheep mentality. Everyone around them teaching them that things can't be done or that they are *"for other people to achieve"*.

Something that would seem insurmountable to an employed person is just a bump to an entrepreneur. Entrepreneurs learn that building problems up in your head to the point where you think you can't do them is a falsehood and they just punch through it. Punch through the excuses. Punch through the obstacles.

"The only thing standing between you and your goal is the bullshit story you keep telling yourself as to why you can't achieve it."
- Jordan Belfort, The Wolf of Wall Street

Entrepreneurs find it easier to separate stress from obstacles. Stress consumes employees, whereas entrepreneurs see it from an analytical standpoint. They say *"How do I get over this or how do we fix this?"* and they **make** the way.

Belief is also about taking in the quiet moments. About really sitting down and understanding that your fears are just feelings and not actual events. That the vast majority of the time those fears never even materialise.

As an entrepreneur you have a lot more time to take stock and think than most people. You're not stuck in a workplace with someone cracking the whip. It's a really busy world out there that is filled, jam packed with pressure and commitments. So, when you roll out of bed and go to work, come home and eat – all you want to do is watch shit on TV and hide from the shitty outside world.

I don't mean hide like a coward. Some people (like me) just aren't wired for the hustle and have to overcome their brain first before they even get into the grind. The amount of mental gymnastics I used to have to do just to stop talking theory every day and get down to business was ridiculous.

My point is, you calm your brain down and escape the stress by watching your favourite show, play your favourite video game. It's ok. It's allowed. It's your choice, you're only human. But evolve past most people by simply admitting that this is the reason you're not achieving what you want.

Hold yourself accountable.

The beneficial flip side of the extra time I have is that I'm constantly collecting my thoughts, never in a rush. YouTube video after YouTube video. Watching hours of video can be perceived as bad, but not if you're watching a podcast and getting a new perspective, or learning business, sales and hustle, watching something on philosophy or human behaviour, or if you're learning more about your industry or skillset. It makes you a much more rounded businessperson and understanding of people, society and structures. You need that brain space, because being a business owner is hard.

People hear that all the time and get discouraged. It's not hard in the way you think it is. When you think of hard - you think of school. I'm not talking about equations, memory etc. I'm talking about:

- Mental toughness.
- Belief.
- Perseverance.
- Setbacks.
- Lows.
- Late payments from multiple clients at once.
- When to hold and when to jump.

- How to deal with people, because some are a nightmare.
- Tolerating.
- Supporting others.
- Seeing the bigger picture.
- Balance.
- When to boast about your ability and achievements and when to show humility.
- Being unable to switch off when you're supposed to be on holiday.
- When to call people out and when to bite your tongue.
- Being surrounded by friends, family and partners and still feeling alone and isolated.
- Dealing with injustices.
- General stress.
- Not really being able to take sick days…

That's how it's hard. Delivering your skill for your clients is just part of it.

Don't get discouraged. Just start. Whenever you can fit it in. People think they can wait until they're the finished article in their head, how the stars will align, and it'll suddenly make sense.

It never happens, you're never the finished article, you're always swimming upstream. It's always hard, just not in the way that you're used to…

…but it's also amazing!

I had a close friend say it's a bit lame to self-identify as an entrepreneur, it made him uncomfortable to do it, that it was something for other people to identify you as if you deserve it. This coming from the same guy who has built a successful business and also hustles other things on the side!

We need to develop more confidence and encourage more people to start, and destroy this shy mindset that people have. The problem isn't the fakes, the problem is the successful are too humble to take ownership of their story, to share it and inspire others. We need to inspire more people to start, and forge the path to Get Unemployed, away from the chains and the hamster wheel, the rolling out of bed to do a job they're forced to do.

> *"You're just a piece of a heartless, shitty machine that makes money."*
> - Joe Rogan

…and it doesn't need to be the millionaires bragging from their mansions. It needs to be those that go out and live their dreams every day, regardless how much money they make.

Look at those in your life that you know are business owners. Are they rocket scientist smart? Are they model good looking? Are they silver spoon, trust fund babies? Are they any number of excuses you can say why they are doing it and you're not? They are not smarter than you. They didn't know something you didn't. They weren't more skilled than you. They took the leap …and that leap is the most exhilarating thing you'll do.

Get out of the mental masturbation and take action.

ACTION

People say:

"I'm too busy for…"

They're not too busy. They're never too busy. There's no such thing as too busy – only excuses. Excuses for not taking the action required. A lot of self-convincing, too. You might be one of those people reading this now. I'm telling you - you're only convincing yourself.

If you want this bad enough, then you're not happy. If you're not happy then you need to find the time to do it, you need to strip back what's making you so busy. If you want it, you'll sleep an hour less at night. If you've got weekend plans, you'll need to do this instead. Got an hour in the car park while you take your kid to Karate? That's your time to work on your business.

You **believe** you're too busy but in reality you're haemorrhaging time all over the place, or you're simply not willing to sacrifice something in your life short term for long term happiness.

How many people say *"my diet's not that bad"* but when it's broken down by anyone that knows about nutrition it becomes apparent it's an absolutely terrible diet.

Be honest with yourself. If you're insecure about how others perceive you that's a completely different conversation, but don't lie to yourself.

Does your current situation disgust you enough yet to leave it behind? Not for a minute, not for an hour, or a day of mental masturbation. Enough that you change …forever. That you make it a choice to commit to this and build it gradually until it becomes full time.

Who says what you're doing now is safe? How many jobs-for-life do you see in this day and age? You think running a business is fragile, you think entrepreneurship is fragile? Employment is fragile. Do you want safety in everything you do?

Safety isn't growth.

There is nothing stopping you. You are a Google search away from doing whatever you want to do. Every answer to any question ever posed in the business world can be answered with a Google search. Consume everything you can, learn in your own time and actually start your business.

College and Universities will need to work harder for signatures in the future. The more people ignore the dogma that *"higher education is the way to riches, freedom and respect"* the more will see that self-education over a shorter period of time can be just, if not more fruitful – without the astronomical debt.

You can learn how to do virtually anything these days, with all the knowledge necessary at your fingertips.

Go do it - because degrees have been sold to you by your government's marketing department. If you want to be a doctor or a lawyer then fair enough, but needless degrees and their associated costs are a waste of time and a scam to burden people with a lifetime of debt.

"I know I want to start a business, but I dunno what."

Are you waiting for me to tell you? You need to decide. I can help you once you're taking action and coming up with problems and questions as a result of that action but I'm not going to draw you a diagram of each step - because it doesn't exist.

It can't exist because there are so many variables, instances, types of people you'll meet and so on. There's no exact process, meaning you'll need to keep falling over. Fall over and learn by yourself, fall over and ask for help.

You can be helped in individual instances, but not given an exact A to B map otherwise *"everyone would be doing it"*.

...and when you start taking action and having these road blocks or failures – no one can say shit because you're the one that's in there taking action! Nobody can say it was handed to you - you went and took it, picking yourself up along the way each time it didn't go smoothly.

I promise, regardless of the grades you've got, the mistakes you've made, the time you have - it's there for the taking. Life rewards action, no exceptions.

The human behaviour behind taking action is actually quite convoluted. In the Coaching space this is understood better than anywhere. Coaches understand that in order for someone to do something, to take the kind of action that changes their life - it has to appear to them that they came up with the solution or decided to do it by themselves.

Coaches (not to be confused with Consultants who **do** advise you) even if they do believe they know the answer, will instead ask questions in such a way that you appear to come to those decisions by yourself. They understand this method is far more effective.

Someone else's opinion makes little effect on someone taking action to better themselves. Telling someone what to do has nothing like the same effect as **discovering** what to do.

As I mentioned earlier, it's one thing reading a book on something like motivation or human behaviour or business or whatever and it's another story altogether *'Getting It'*.

You can read whatever book cover to cover and there's not a sentence you don't understand. You understand the concept, ethos, facts and so on …but there's something different that happens when you actually start doing it …living it.

That's when the real light bulb moment comes on and you're like:

"…fuck, they really were right!"

You take it with you, now internalised and it influences every decision you make, every conversation you have. It's like magic. You understood it before but now you **get it!** It's not until you actively go out and do things that you will become hard-wired.

You cannot learn or internalise this without taking action. If you want to make the right decisions on autopilot, it firstly takes years of being *'in it'*. Once you do that though, you stop second guessing yourself, which is great if you're typically used to deliberating and stressing about making the right decisions in your life. I get asked by my clients *"What should I do here? What should I say here? How should I approach this?"*. This is from smart people, typically smarter than me, and it never fails to surprise me how far I've come that I can answer for them, every time.

What's the moral of this? Someone commanding you to take action isn't as effective as wanting to do it yourself. I can't force my clients to do something they don't want to do because the result will be lousy. We can come to an agreement on what they want, and I can hold them accountable to get things done. Things happen much quicker and to a higher standard that way.

Speaking of action…

TO FINISH THIS SECTION

I'm only interested in truth. In helping you through the truth. You should focus on the truth at all times. People get wrapped up in motivational, cute, touchy feely bullshit that tells them to follow their dreams, everything's going to be ok, you're powerful etc.

These things are fine, as long as they have context and are explained with tough love. Nobody owes you a thing. Effort and persistence are the only things that are important. Unfortunately, that doesn't sell books or help motivational videos get views, because it's the flip side to all the good things you want to mentally masturbate over, but then go back to the life that you want to change, but never do.

The Inspiration and the *'How To'* are both important.

The inspiration is what's going to make you do it. The *'How To'* is how you get it done. The problem at the moment is that all the advice out there is just inspiration. The gurus getting the big numbers, the views, the likes, the shares - it's because they're only selling the inspiration. The problem with inspiration **only** is that it's permanent mental masturbation.

The belief that:

"I will get round to it."

"When I do decide to take action, it'll be waiting there for me."

The *'How To'* needs to exist - it might be the more tedious to watch, focus on, take the time out to look at, and it's definitely the least glamorous ...but it's the one that's going to make the difference.

You can spend your whole life reading books, watching motivational YouTube videos and attending seminars, but every time you find the next thing you think you need to consume that'll solve your problem – it's putting a stop to taking action. You end up in this perpetual state of consuming information and never taking that action.

It's amazing how much more often your phone goes when you're perceived as successful. There's no shortage of people wanting to go for a coffee and pick your brains, disguised as a *'catch-up'*. A few times I've even somehow ended up paying! Even though I tell them how to do it, they stay in the cycle – you'll tell them how you did it, but they'll be dissatisfied that the truth is hard work, failing and perseverance. Like you're not telling them the *"one simple trick"* to do it themselves easily.

If you ask for a meeting with someone to pick their brains about business (or anything), at least be honest and value their time. Much like business - begin with firstly thinking about how you can give the other person value. They probably don't need anything from you, but it makes the whole situation less selfish …and doesn't help feed my misanthropy.

This perpetual state of only consuming and never taking action is your brain's way of protecting you. It stops you putting yourself out there so that you can't fail at it then feel bad and ashamed. You can hide away in your comfort zone, consume the content and say *"this makes sense, that makes sense, won't it be great when I start this?"*

…then you never actually start.

There is no substitute for action. There is no instruction you can be given in a book that's more effective than going out and taking the action yourself and learning on your feet.

It's the same principal as going to study for several years, only for employers to turn around and say *"You must have X years' experience"* or *"You must have experience in a similar role"*.

Taking action and learning from experience trumps it all. If you're afraid of failing, it doesn't matter - you can be the most prepared person that ever was and there will still be unique situations and eventualities that come up along the way that you didn't anticipate.

So, if you're going to fuck up anyway, you might as well be doing the *"learning on your feet"* kind of fucking up instead of spending your whole life in that comfort zone coming up with solutions to fake scenarios.

Learn on your feet **earlier**, so at least you've started earlier, so that you're further ahead than you would have been hiding away and planning.

I did the same thing, and my only regret is I didn't start sooner.

Graeme Lawson

"If you're not doing what you love, you're wasting your time"
- Billy Joel

BUSINESS

CONGRATULATIONS!

You've started (or have been thinking about starting) a business:

- No more office politics.
- No more worrying about what you say.
- No more commute.
- No more humouring people you don't like.

You now choose who to deal with and what you're willing to put up with. Never again pander to douche bags or put up with ass kissers, back stabbers, drama queens, gossip, office affairs and the endless supply of annoying people.

Nothing you do needs to involve anyone that you're not comfortable dealing with.

Think about that for a second, everyone you deal with in your working life, from colleagues to customers - getting to keep the good ones and dropping the bad ones. Never having a boss again or holding your tongue when someone does something you're unhappy with.

It's your business – you're in charge of everything. It's liberating, it's freedom and it's **taking control**.

…but something happened a generation or so ago…

BUSINESS NOW VS BUSINESS THEN

From the dawn of human beings, we began communicating and converging into small tribes. Once we discovered this was far more effective than everyone attempting to survive individually, small communities sprung up in which everyone played their part. Man hunts and protects, women produce and nurture children. Everyone comes together in the preservation of the tribe and the protection from threats like other tribes and dangerous animals.

Then, as we became more civilised, we were able to trade. One person fishes, another can build shelter – a deal is done trading X amount of fish for someone building a hut. Everyone is self-sufficient and survival is built around what you can offer, your skillset and the infrastructure you've built for yourself. Naturally more skilled trades and higher value or rarer products commanded better trading power.

Then money, or currency was introduced, allowing for more regulation or standard of what something is worth.

However, something happened around the industrial revolution where the general public were farmed to fill roles instead of being self-employed, and we've never really recovered.

How normal does it seem to go into education from a young age, sit like a good little drone in a classroom for years until you discover what you have an aptitude for, graduate then head off, clocking into your 9 to 5 every day, working for 'The Man'. This is what is seen as normal these days.

Churning the working class through this system is the new norm.

Running your own business is relatively rare these days (or even having a trade). You only need to go back to the start of my parent's generation where a quarter of people ran their own business! The establishment have engineered the system just how they want it – workers willing to do the work under poorer and poorer circumstances for their profit.

That worked fine for a while, until they got greedier and greedier. Nowadays the average worker is squeezed, working well over 40 hours is the norm, house prices, food and fuel have gone up way, way past inflation salary increases, their pensions aren't worth anything like what past retirees were getting. In fact, a state pension might not even exist by the time those starting out today are due to retire.

Corporate greed has the ratio from the lowest earner in a company to CEO from 40 times the salary previously to 300 times the salary today! We have food banks in 2019 because some workers in full time employment can't even afford to feed their families.

Think you're safe investing in your own portfolio? They have recessions and financial crisis's cropping up a few times per lifetime to cover that, too.

So, what happened? You've been duped into working for *The Man*, getting paid shit and saving for a pension that you pray you get to see when you retire.

They've even peddled the mantra that working your fingers bloody for someone else is a noble pursuit. Getting into work earlier than everyone else, leaving later than everyone else, getting double time working the weekend:

"I know what a hard days' work is, boy!".

Imagine bragging about how much more time you spent in the yard or in the office. Bragging about doing something you fucking hate for longer than everyone else…

How duped are you?

THE ALTERNATIVE

Be your own boss. The master of your own destiny. Answer to no one. Own your life. Don't take shit from anyone and don't ever again need anything so bad that you can't walk away.

You have full control of your life. Full responsibility of whether it works or fails. If you fuck it up - who's going to say something? ...and if they do - who cares? You dared while they stayed on the shore and hid from the rapids.

You dust yourself off and go again.

The people that actually matter will admire you, I promise. But most importantly, don't do it for them - do it for yourself. If you fuck up - it's because of you. When you **win** - it's because of you! ...and you get to fuck up as many times as you need to before you win.

You get one shot at life. The world is amazing, with great places, people and experiences. Who wants to spend it trading 5 days at work, with all the office politics and afraid-to-say-the-wrong-thing drones for 2 days of freedom?

You're then expected to squirrel away a lump of cash every month for a pension, plus investments - then the government tells you you're getting less than you planned, *"Sorry you'll have to work longer, the stock market crashed - you lost your investments"* ...or something happens and you die before you even get to see any of it, you squirrel your shit away and work like a carthorse all of your life for nothing!

Take control and don't leave anything in anyone else's hands. You can't put a price on the peace of mind this brings.

You have knowledge and it's up to you what you do with it.

- You can get a job with it.
- You can build a business trading that knowledge for money.

- You can improve on that knowledge, get better results and charge higher fees.
- You can teach that knowledge.
- You can leverage that knowledge by creating passive systems.

…or you can do nothing with it.

You can make a success of any business …**any business**, with enough persistence.

Not intelligence or talent, but persistence. If you persist for long enough, you'll be listening to the market and making the subtle (or not so subtle) changes needed to make your business meet those market needs.

Adapt or die.

Why did Blockbuster lose out to online video streaming services like Netflix? Why did HMV lose out to online music streamers like Spotify? Why did Toys 'R' Us lose out to the likes of Amazon? Inability to adapt. In the case of those 3 examples - it was underestimating the consumers obsession with convenience.

You **must** listen to the market. Not your mum, not Jimmy down the pub – the market. Your customers, your potential customers, what your competitors are having success with, what leaders in your industry are teaching, what technology is being invented. This principal is the same regardless if you're a property developer …or if you trim hedges part-time.

Think about it: You could start with the shittest idea, everyone's telling you it won't work, you're losing out on customers – but you're willing to adapt, to make anything from a slight tinker to a seismic shift in how you operate by **listening** to those around you that you want to sell to.

"A pessimist sees the difficulty in every opportunity; an optimist sees the opportunity in every difficulty."
- Winston Churchill

All of a sudden that shitty idea is a massive success because you **listened** to what the market demanded, and you made the necessary adjustments.

You sold people what they wanted. That's all business is: Product or service meeting demand.

I don't care how much you doubt yourself, if you can do this then you can run any business. It doesn't matter what the discipline is or at what stage you're at. Going for the sale, designing a product or speaking at an event – build it around what people want, listen to them, not what you want to sell them.

PERSONAL BRANDING VS BUSINESS BRANDING

When you start a business, a decision has to be made:

- Do I create a personal brand?
- Do I call my business a name?

Both have their positives and negatives, some obvious, some less so. Your personal brand is around you personally - like I do with my business. A business brand is usually an identity that doesn't mention you directly – you are part of the business rather than being the business, so to speak.

Although in a lot of cases it can seem much of a muchness – there are some key reasons to consider before you start:

- Would you prefer to be hidden from the images the company promotes, regardless if a personal brand makes more sense on paper? You might not have the stomach to be seen or value your privacy in a big way.

- Do you want to use your personal social media accounts or are you creating new ones that are the business name? You're looking to build up a bank of historic content, so getting this right from the start is important. Do your current social accounts have pictures of you falling out of bars at 1am – does that look bad, particularly in your industry? Do you care?

- Do you see this as a pathway launching your own private speaking career, to be invited onto podcasts, talk shows or speaking gigs? It's a lot easier to be the famous John Smith, rather than John Smith of the famous ACME Widgets.

- Do you want the perception of a big company, or have the funding to start big from scratch? Perception of size might be important in your industry.

- Do you have an exit strategy? Are there ambitions to grow and sell the business at some point? Investors can't buy you, so you'll need a tangible asset, intellectual property and good will to go along with the sale.

In my own business, my clients know when they use me, they get me - because my name's on the door. Would they know that anyway if my company was called *"Chocolate Starfish Media"*? Yeah, sure - but it's subliminal. I want my clients to know that when they sign up - they will get me and no one else, and that it will never change …not part of an agency where they become *'just another account'* and most of their work is passed on to a junior.

It wasn't created out of narcissism, it was a case of: I don't plan to own an agency, so I don't need it to look like I have a bigger company than I do. I don't have premises or an overly-intellectualised logo, so I might as well articulate that by having my name on the door.

It also allowed me to put my personality out there and not worry if it hurt this fictional brand. If someone didn't like me, they just didn't work with me – which suits us both.

My name and tagline is currently:

Graeme Lawson
Digital Marketing & Business Growth

The tagline tells you what you need to know, so I don't need a company name.

There's also nothing wrong with building a company and not being the face of it, enjoying your privacy and not having one of those team pages that tell you *'Peter likes playing Minecraft and brewing his own beer between projects"* and *'Helen likes watching The Great British Bake Off at the weekend when she's not entertaining her grandchildren."*

…and get your fucking dog off of your team page.

Yes, people buy from people, so you need to humanise your brand in some way – preferably not with one of those pages, though.

It's also important to consider what would happen if you want to go in a different direction. If you **are** your brand then your name is of course tied to you, not the service – making the transition easy. However, if you have a business name, that name might be associated with that service, either literally or what you've built it up as – do you sell the asset and start another business from scratch? Do you pay someone else to run it and start something else? Can you open your new direction as a *'wing'* of that existing business?

There are many options. I always lean on the personal brand because that never goes away – but it might not suit your personal preference, your industry or the size of the fish you think you need a business brand to catch.

MORE ON: TIME OVER MONEY

Back to the *"Working your fingers to the bone is noble"* thing again. The great thing about running a business is understanding time and money.

Having a life is important. I don't want to name names because, well, they're doing their thing, but a lot of the bigger influencers in the motivational space talk about getting your head down and forgoing having fun for a period of time. Like:

"Eat shit in your 20's but live the rest of your life rich!"

I'd hate to think about all the fun shit I would've missed out on in my 20's. A lot of the time I was broke, but I was having the time of my life! I had great nights out, great nights in, great times and experiences and trips with friends, great relationships, and I wouldn't swap that for 100% guaranteed comfort now. No way! It was too good.

Not only that - if I hustled that hard and delved deep for that long it would create a hardwired habit that would be very hard to decompress from. I wouldn't find myself in my 30's on the beach sipping cocktails, even if I'd made enough to do so. The grind would become me, consume me and would sacrifice the level of relationship I have with others, my downtime, my mental health. I'd be estranged and socially awkward.

"Beware the barrenness of a busy life."
- Socrates

Time is more important than money. Money is in abundance. I appreciate when you don't have it, it certainly doesn't feel that way, but in life, money is abundant. You can always earn more, but you cannot use it to buy more time. Time is the most important thing in the world.

I'm not talking about never eating cake, having a beer or whatever your vice is so you can live to 150. Not the time at the back-end of your life, I'm talking about the day-to-day throughout all of your adulthood.

They say too much of anything is bad for you, it's the same with work. Working **in** your business, not lifting your head up to work **on** your business makes you blinkered, stresses you and ages you. Don't let anyone bully you or shame you into sacrificing your physical or mental health by working your fingers to the bone.

*"I don't have time for growth, I'm really busy working **in** my business."*

Yes, your business hours may be jam packed, but you **must** push through this excuse and work **on** your business, even if it means at undesirable hours. That might mean before or after work, it might be the weekend. I could say:

"Things have been going so well with the business, I've not made time to write my book!"

Which could be seen as true because things **have** been going so well with my business for a long time now. But the truth would be that I don't want to finish it enough if I'm not willing to work on it outside running the business.

Running a business allows you to improve on the skills you already have, meaning you can charge more for your time and then eventually create passive income streams that stop you trading time for money. You have value and how you utilise this is vitally important. It is the difference between running a business and clocking in as a glorified employee.

PROVIDING VALUE

As I touched on before: Adapting and thus providing value for your customers is the only thing that ultimately matters.

- What happened in Social Media's entire existence when anyone whined about a high-profile political topic? Absolutely nothing.
- What happens when you whine about Brexit on Twitter? Absolutely nothing.
- What happens when you whine about Donald Trump on Facebook? Absolutely nothing.
- What happens when anyone whines about anything? Absolutely nothing.

Nobody's listening, nobody cares, other than your gormless, sycophantic, confirmation bias friends who have something new to circle jerk over.

You're not changing the world, you're not contributing anything other than your shitty, boring opinion, just like all the other shitty, boring opinions that clog up the internet and avoid creating any real progress. Roll up your sleeves and either get on with it or fix it.

PRO-TIP: Whining on Facebook won't do it.

Business is exactly the same. You can't complain your way out of it, you have to fix it. The law of supply and demand dictates it. Shit businesses that don't adapt - die as they should. The market is the same as natural selection.

The blame is yours alone.

People think they are entitled to a job, but do you know how you get a job? Being an asset to a business. Any job you have has to turn a business owner a profit. Know when you're not an asset? When another 10,000 people behind you can do the same job. Know what's happening when there's 10,000 people going for the same job? There aren't enough jobs ...because not enough people are running businesses.

Not so long ago a quarter of people were self-employed, now it's more like 15% in the UK and 6% in the United States! The education system is rigged to get you into a 9 to 5 job, yet it is **proven** that the self-employed are what kept the economy afloat and helped us bounce back quicker from the recent recession.

With the internet, you have the entire world at your fingertips to train yourself in something completely different, allowing you to earn a job or start a business. This is an unprecedented situation in history. There is no excuse. I use the term *'earn a job'* deliberately because you are not owed a job by anyone. You must be an irreplaceable asset.

Regardless of how shit a government is, there is no one stopping you becoming an irreplaceable asset other than the person looking back at you in the mirror.

Businesses are not charities – you are not owed a job. You must provide Return On Investment (ROI). Even businesses that are literally charities need an ROI on you!

Here's an extreme example of how to provide value and become an irreplaceable asset:

Let's say Jim and Emma are a couple that stay in a relatively small community and want to go out for dinner, but they need a babysitter for their kid, Joe.

A friend of the couple has a daughter, Lucy who can babysit. Lucy meets with the couple; she seems nice and they decide to give her the regular gig.

One day, while browsing YouTube, Lucy notices a video *"Social Media for Small Business"*. She watches the video, which leads to another video …and so on:

"Man, I could totally do that!"

…she thinks to herself as she consumes and learns more and more of the information.

Lucy arrives at Jim and Emma's house one day, ready to babysit. Jim and Emma are talking to each other about their accounting firm and how they could really be doing with more business.

Overhearing, Lucy explains she's been researching how to find new customers, engage with existing ones and increase companies' awareness through social media. She says she can work on it a little bit at a time, after she puts Joe to bed.

Jim and Emma's firm don't really have a social media strategy, so they decide to give it a shot - they've got nothing to lose.

Lucy gains access to the firms' social accounts, strategises the type of content she wants to post (which we'll cover in the Marketing section), puts a posting plan together and gets to work!

After a few weeks, Jim and Emma notice the increased engagement on their firms' social platforms, they've even had calls from small business owners in the area who've seen the firms posts which, now as new clients, convert to thousands in additional revenue per year.

OK, so initially, even in a small community where there must be dozens of babysitters that could replace Lucy - do you think she would be replaced now? Even if she couldn't do one of the nights Jim and Emma wanted?

No!

She increased her value and made herself an irreplaceable asset. Not only this: Jim and Emma now also pay Lucy a **lot** more than a typical babysitter.

Lucy could then take what worked in that campaign and:

- Branch out to other businesses.
- Specialise in accounting firms in her area, then her country, then all over the world.
- Ask Jim and Emma to recommend their business friends.
- Use the couple as a case study or testimonial.
- Get results for many more businesses then write a book, or start a blog, or a YouTube channel, or be a guest speaker - all helping businesses improve their social media presence.
- Train others and then start an agency with a team.

All because she's proven her value. All because she researched. All because she took that opportunity when being present during Jim and Emma's conversation.

'Adapting & Providing Value'
...get that tattooed on your face.

If you are employed or going for a job, how are you providing value? What sets you apart from others going for that same job or stopping you from being replaced?

If you're running a business, what value are you giving to your customers that others around you are not? You are not owed a job or customers. You provide value over and above the hundreds or thousands of others vying for that business owners' attention.

Be useful. Rather than being a structured drone - bring value to the world. Could you imagine the impact if everyone did this? Could you imagine you in your dying days knowing that you made a measurable difference to people with your product or service, that you made at least a fleeting mark on the world? Take responsibility for it and make it happen. Not for toys and trinkets - for the betterment of your own self and for other people.

Do something of value: It's more rewarding and it gives something to the world.

I've never been interested in playing the markets or investments etc. It might be something you're genuinely interested in as a passion, it might be how you afford your freedom, but shifting numbers around on the screen – while there is a ton of skill and persistence involved, it provides nothing but making money.

Yes, sometimes I'm making rich people richer with my skillset, but most of the time I'm growing small businesses. Helping a client grow their business lets them relax a little more instead of being hand-to-mouth. Maybe they have a well-deserved holiday after years of constantly building something, maybe they can finally justify growing their family, maybe they provide a great service that their customers truly benefit from. Sometimes I'm encouraging people to start their business, follow their dreams and ambitions. It all has tangible value.

Everyone should be putting something of value in that helps a functioning society flourish.

VALUE VS EDUCATION

You don't need a degree. Get so good at something and you will be hired. Get hired or win a client by **showing how good you are**, not by holding up a bit of paper.

Ability is more important than degrees. People buy based on ability, not education.

You know what I'd be doing if I wanted to be a videographer? I'd go out and film a bunch of footage then lock myself in my room, and I wouldn't come out until I edited the shit out of the film. I'd study other films I liked online and then Google and YouTube how to create those same effects I liked. I'd join forums and see what others are doing and I'd maybe buy a course…

…and I'd do that over and over again.

I'd probably be really proud of the first few videos I produced, but I'd get progressively better. I'd probably look back at those videos 3 years later and decide that they were actually a bit shit. Because everyone's a bit shit when they first start something, but they get better in such a progressive way they can't see those improvements until they take a look back at much earlier work.

Then, when I reach the point where I'm great at it, I'd go for a job and say:

"Here's my hard work, here's my standard, here's what I busted my ass to learn and I'm completely self-taught."

Not *"Here's my degree - give me a job"*. You don't need the degree and the debt. You need the proof to be in your work, the dirt under your fingernails, the effort and the sacrifice.

Or, preferably use those new skills to start your own business.

If someone goes on to university for 3 or 4 years and becomes, say, a personal trainer - I still might charge twice as much per hour as them. Then...

- There will be someone that does the same thing as me but charges twice as much as I do.
- There will be top surgeons who charge ten times more than me.
- There will be those that do the same thing as me but charge ten times more than those surgeons!

The point is your value, your positioning in the market and what that market's willing to pay for it.

Business is not rigid. That's why it's hard to earn a business degree and knock it out of the park right away. Nothing is factual, situations have instances, their own idiosyncrasies and most importantly - people. Things you just can't learn in a textbook, you have to **go out and do it**. Trial and error. Which brings me back to action and value...

You cannot sell to your clients what **you** want to sell them. You have to solve a problem or fulfil a need for them – a fix for what they think is broken. Winging it completely with clients is unacceptable but you must start at a certain point of skill or service, sooner rather than later and be ready to move in the direction the market demands, engineering it as you go. All the preparation and theory is pointless without action.

If you need to charge less than you planned to get those initial customers through the door and hone the service - fine. If you need to offer those services for free to the right people - fine. Do whatever it takes.

This gives you the opportunity to kill it for those clients, build up an understanding of what you did well, what you could improve on, how it compares to what your competition is offering, how you can do things better than the competition, what you can add to your service that your competitors are not, get testimonials, case studies to show other potential customers, and so on.

As soon as you have proof that you provided value to one customer, you can then show other potential customers who are in the same position as that customer once was before you started working with them. If one person needed it - others will too, and you will be armed with not only proof but a better understanding of what to do next time. Build on this with each one.

Take that action, make those necessary changes, show others your proof.

BUSINESS OWNERS AND GOALS

Businesses Are Not Run By The Smartest People.

Dramatic clickbait headline!

When I was a kid growing up, I thought the Prime Minister of the UK and the President of the United States (or any head of any country) had to be the nicest and smartest people in the world due to that position's importance.

I thought police officers had to be the toughest and bravest, with some of the best people skills. I thought lawyers had to have the highest moral fibre to make sure *'the right thing'* always happened.

It makes the most sense to put all those people in each of those roles …but that's not necessarily the case. Just as this is true for those roles, it's also true for business owners, who I assumed must be some of the smartest people alive!

Business looks hard. It's portrayed as 3-piece suits and ties, shiny pens in large boardrooms and big brains to cope with difficult business decisions, employing people and building something from nothing into a success.

It doesn't work like that. Of course, it's hard in many ways, but as discussed in the previous section – anyone can do it. I work with people every day that are particularly skilful in their field but by their own admission – suck at business. That can be overcome with time and persistence, a willingness to learn or they pay someone like me to help them run it more effectively, efficiently, win more clients, attract a better standard of client and so on. There is always a solution.

I also work with those that aren't skilled in a traditional craft but are great business owners, organisers of others, leaders of men and women that build fantastic, successful businesses.

Learn your strengths. Know your strengths. Play to your strengths. Recruit those who help supplement your weaknesses or train your own weaknesses.

So, now you know you can do it – what do you want to achieve? It's hard enough getting over that first hurdle of believing you're even worthy of starting – so what's next?

With all the gurus in the *"I run a business exclusively selling ~~suckers~~ other people information products on how to run a business without ever actually having real experience running one myself"* boasting things like *"6 Figure Business Guide"* and *"7 Figure Master Plan"*, it's really hard to get a firm grasp on what's achievable and setting realistic goals.

If you're currently working in a job, haven't started a business yet or don't make a lot in your current business - that shit might be cool to click on at first and read for a bit, but it's too daunting, you just can't see where that happens short term. I left a well-paid job, but I remember thinking *"Man, if I can just make 2k per month that would cover everything comfortably"*.

- Maybe you live with your parents and 1k is good?
- Maybe 500 is good?
- But maybe you need 10k a month to replace your current salary?

Everyone's circumstances are different. The biggest achievement is proving to yourself that you can do it. After you make your first sale selling your service, delivering that service and getting paid for it, making your money completely off your own back is incredible! The rest of your business is just scaling that thing you did.

It's great saying: *"Yeah but you should set your targets big! Shoot for 7 figures! And if you only make 6 you're all good!"*

It doesn't work if that makes you disillusioned from the start, afraid to even begin because you might fail. Focus on making your initial targets a little out of your comfort zone. Work out the end result you want, then work back from there as to what incremental goals it's going to take to get there. Then just make sure you do the work and actually go out and get it!

"Between stimulus and response, there is a space. In that space is our power to choose our response. In our response lies our growth and our freedom."
- Victor Franki

In any instance (and what I teach all my clients) - resist the urge to ever take the easy way out. Speaking from experience as someone who never cut corners, who never sold something I couldn't fulfil – life is much, much easier that way. I cannot tell you the grief you will endure, as I see it every day from those who either scam or blag what they're capable of …and quite frankly, it cannot possibly be worth it.

Never mind the reputation damage, never mind the moral dilemma of even doing anything underhand in the first place – life is too short and mental health is too valuable. Don't give in to any urges, don't take the easy way out. Building your business ethically is where the personal growth is and it's where the satisfaction exists, knowing you'll always have your integrity.

Business is mentally tough enough without skeletons in your closet holding you back and keeping you awake at night.

Speaking of mentally tough enough – get your processes in place! By that I mean streamline everything that you can, put systems in place, get notes out of your head and write them down.

"Business is easy; people are difficult."
- Duncan Bannatyne

Yes, people can be difficult – both intentionally and unwittingly. People don't care about you. They care about themselves. Paying you is not a priority. Their priorities are servicing existing clients and finding new clients. You don't feature. You are an inconvenience. I learned this the hard way and it's why for years now I've only dealt in automatic payments. No invoicing late and hoping clients pay on time.

Speaking of time - mine is too valuable. I refuse to spend it sending invoices and worrying about getting paid. My service is good and reasonably priced - I deserve to be paid on time.

I remember vividly being owed around £6,000 from various clients at one time and yet I had literally nothing in the bank, with my overdraft maxed. I came out of a meeting and put my bank card in the machine to pay for my parking ticket, but it declined. I turned around to the two ladies in the queue behind me and said *"Sorry, I don't know why it won't take my card and I've got no change on me"*. I was about to step aside and work out what to do next, but these two ladies just laughed and said *"Don't be silly, we'll pay your ticket for you, son"*. When I asked for a phone number or email to get the money back to them, they just laughed and said they were *"Paying It Forward"*.

The kindness over a £3.70 parking fee was amazing, but I have to be honest, once I checked the online banking on my phone and saw there was actually nothing there:

I don't think I've ever felt so worthless.

I wasn't getting paid on time, and while this can be considered normal, I felt like I wasn't respected enough, that my work wasn't good enough. That if I demanded to be paid it would cause friction and not only would I still not be paid – but I'd lose the clients also.

This is just one example of where I had to refine my process, but it was four years before I had it properly implemented.

Having things like this in place is the difference for someone like me being able to travel and not. It's the sort of thing that if I had the confidence and the conviction to implement from the start - I would've saved years of drama. Learn from my mistakes.

"We Succeed Through Trial and Error, Not Hopes and Dreams."
- Me

It was freezing – really fucking freezing. Demoralising. Miles out of my comfort zone.

Me and my buddy Craig had an *"amazing"* idea in January 2012. We were going to sell advertising space on an A4 leaflet. This leaflet would:

- Go out to 10,000 homes in radius of the businesses we were speaking to. Potential customers could cut out a coupon and present it to the business.
- Have a custom QR Code that linked to a section of a website I'd designed, dedicated to the area where all the businesses were located. They would have their own mobile responsive landing page that collected the customer data for list building (bearing in mind this was 2012, so very up to date stuff). Meaning the old school could cut out the coupon, but the more tech savvy could use the QR Code.
- I'd also rank the website to be number one on Google for the area we were targeting.

So, I went to Royal Mail… far too expensive. One of my contacts put me in touch with a company that specialised in this sort of thing. I met with them and they could do it for half what Royal Mail were charging. Not only was it half, it included the printing too!

We picked one of the most famous streets in Glasgow, awash with businesses, popular with students and the middle class. The street was searched for over 20,000 times a month on Google - so good for ranking. The street was also over half a mile long, so would take some time walking the full length, stopping at virtually every business on the way down on both sides of the road to ask if they were interested.

I'd designed an example landing page of what the business would get, loaded it up on my phone and we hit the street!

It took us over 3 hours. Going into each shop, asking to speak to the owner or manager, showing them the product and explaining it to them in detail. That we were local business owners and that this was going to reach tens of thousands of people.

...I thought it was a no-brainer.

We spoke to only one business **owner** the whole time.

One!

(I mean, admittedly, he did say he was very interested)

I guessed business owners weren't that involved in the direct running of high-end shops. Most managers we spoke to were able to give us the details of the owner in some shape or form. If I remember right, we got 18 personal email addresses.

Next, we borrowed an office to record a personalised video for each of those emails. 18 videos, all explaining that we were in their shop that day, who we spoke to, what the product was and how much exposure and reach they would get.

To summarise:

- At least 2 meetings with me and Craig discussing and planning the idea.
- Designed a mock-up leaflet.
- Designed the website with a separate mock up mobile landing page and QR Code.
- Had a meeting with the leaflet distributer and printer.
- Spent over 3 hours, not including travel, to walk the length of the half mile street, in a typical Scottish January.
- Borrowed an office to film 18 personalised videos, edit them and upload them to YouTube and then send it out to those 18 email addresses.

Can you tell how many sign ups we had?

One *"possibly interested"*.

If I'd continued to hope and dream about starting my own business (took me 6 years of dreaming before I pulled the trigger)...

If I'd listened to my boss at the time who told me to *"Start looking to climb the ladder within the company and stop all this 'I'm going to run my own business' nonsense"*...

If I'd listened to well-meaning friends that told me quitting my well-paid job in a recession was a bad idea...

If I'd just read books on how to run my business instead of making hilarious fuck ups like the story above...

I wouldn't be where I am today.

I've worked with many big companies and projects on my business journey but none that would've happened if I hadn't accepted that we succeed through trial and error, not hopes and dreams. It's important to hope and dream, but it's worthless if you don't step into the arena, willing to try and fail.

"26 times I've been trusted to take the game winning shot and missed. I've failed over and over and over again in my life ...and that is why I succeed."
- Michael Jordan

If I'd allowed others to deter me, to make me give up or to keep me in my comfort zone, only hoping to make micro improvements every so often I wouldn't be where I am today.

Remember: This makes a good story to tell now, and looking back it was a good lesson for me – but it didn't feel like that at the time and I had no idea what that kind of behaviour and persistence would lead to. That's the secret – not knowing at the time, not having the hindsight, but doing it anyway with the belief that you won't be stacking failures upon failures forever.

Want to hear the opposite result of a story like that?

Part of the digging holes for my step brothers fencing company I talked about in this book's intro also had me helping occasionally with *'other jobs'* like fitting floors. One of those days we went to pick up laminate flooring from a very large Scottish supplier, with several stores nationwide.

I overheard the owner talking to my step brother about how they were doing really well locally around each store, but they weren't making a dent online, even though their infrastructure often dwarfed their UK wide competitors who were cleaning up on Google.

I held my tongue at the time. I didn't think he would take the guy with the scabby jeans labouring for some guy that regularly buys his laminate flooring seriously. So, I left and had a think about what the owner had said and fantasised about how big a deal that would be.

Anyway, I procrastinated on it for a few weeks until one day I spotted the owner heading in the opposite direction from me in his Porsche towards one of his stores. I decided in that moment I was going to stop overthinking things, how I would approach him, what I would say and so on and I spun my car around at the roundabout and went after him.

I pulled up outside his store, walked over to his car and knocked on the window, not realising he hadn't left the car because he was on hands free talking to someone!

Good start.

He was cool about it and I explained who I was, the conversation I was privy to and how I felt I could help him, asking how he was doing with his Search Engine Optimisation (SEO). He explained he knew what that was, but they hadn't tried it. The whole time I was waiting for him to remember me as the scruffy dude, wet from that rainy day buying laminate and say:

"Thanks, but no thanks."

On the spot I decided I didn't have enough proof or leverage in my own ability for a project that size that he would take seriously, so as casually as I could, I asked:

"Why don't you let me do it for a month for free and I'll show you what I can do?"

It was a no brainer and he agreed to have a sit-down meeting one month later to talk about the results.

Within a month I moved them from relative obscurity onto the first page of Google for their local terms and made a huge dent on improving their UK wide search terms. They didn't even flinch at my retainer, which despite the fact I'd been in business less than a year at that point (over 7 years ago now) was still a huge chunk of money, even by my standards today.

Fast forward three months and I had them 3rd in the whole of the UK for anyone searching *"Laminate Flooring"* on Google, along with many other search terms. The difference in their online sales were astronomical and they were suddenly competing with the big UK suppliers.

Around that time my stepbrother was in the store again, buying more laminate and he asked a member of staff how things were going. They said:

"It's been quiet in the store lately, but online sales have gone crazy!"

I love both of those stories as they remind me of how much effort can be put in for potentially no reward and how another spur of the moment decision can go on to mean so much.

As I mentioned in the previous section about luck:

- Firstly, I had to quit my job and start the business.
- I had to be willing to lose my savings and go broke without a job.
- I had to work side jobs to keep myself afloat.
- While working a side job I took advantage of a conversation I overheard and ultimately chased down the owner in my car in a sort of *'now or never'* moment.
- I made him an offer he couldn't refuse.
- I worked that month for free just to prove I could do it.

- I met with the owner and showed him my results, which were awesome.
- I then got my first big contract.

Lucky break, huh.

I discovered a need, I tabled a fix for the need, including an irresistible offer. I provided immense value and that built trust.

I always start off offering a new service much cheaper, it allows me to get clients in and improve on the skill in real time. Then once you know you're delivering great value, you can increase the price to your more preferable rate.

Price lower for experience, for testimonials and case studies. Don't be greedy. If you're truly providing great value (which should be the goal of every business) then you'll win more business as a result and increase your prices from there.

This is important to understand early, as it has a compound effect. Your business and marketing efforts work much like the *'doubling every day'* analogy, starting with a penny:

Day 1 is **1p**
Day 2 is **2p**
Day 3 is **4p**
Day 4 is **8p**
Day 5 is **16p**
Day 6 is **32p**
Day 7 is **64p**
Day 8 is **£1.28**

This is taking forever!

Day 9 is **£2.56**
Day 10 is **£5.12**
Day 11 is **£10.24**
Day 12 is **£20.48**
Day 13 is **£40.96**
Day 14 is **£81.92**
Day 15 is **£163.84**

15 days just to break £100?!

Day 16 is **£327.68**
Day 17 is **£655.36**
Day 18 is **£1,310.72**
Day 19 is **£2,621.44**
Day 20 is **£5,242.88**
Day 21 is **£10,485.76**

Wait, what's happening here? 15 days to break £100 but only another 6 to get over 10k?

Day 22 is **£20,971.52**
Day 23 is **£41,943.04**
Day 24 is **£83,886.08**
Day 25 is **£167,772.16**

Another 4 days now has us well over 100k!

Day 26 is **£335,544.32**
Day 27 is **£671,088.64**
Day 28 is **£1,342,177.28**

A further 3 days and we've cracked a million!

Day 29 is **£2,684,354.56**
Day 30 is **£5,368,709.12**
Day 31 is **£10,737,418.24**

The final 3 days takes us over 10 million, just by doubling every day for 31 days, having started with a penny!

Treat your business, your marketing efforts, your interactions, the thankless tasks you perform, the ideas you have, the learning you do, the good work you do every day like this analogy.

It may feel like you're getting nowhere or making very little progress in the beginning but the compound effect of it can't be ignored. I see it every day in my own work and with my clients. If it's business advice, marketing efforts or just accountability – pushing them every week to keep going makes them grow slowly but surely …but once they crack it, things speed up!

Micro improvements make it hard to see the progress you're making. Sometimes even big achievements seem caveated:

- Maybe you got to work with a huge client but it's under the veil of another company.

- Maybe you got the premises you always wanted but you have to partner up or take a risky investment to afford it.

- Maybe you started your business so that one day you could walk into a Ferrari dealership and buy a new car, but you've settled for a 10-year-old second hand one instead.

With a combination of the micro achievements and the caveated big ones - you look back over the last 5 years and everything you've done and achieved is unrecognisable from where you started. You get better and better, the existing caveats disappear, new ones arrive - but it always gets better.

Never give up on trying new things and exploring new directions. I failed plenty of times for various reasons, and as I explained in the first section – if you try in 100 different instances and 90 of them fail – you're still 10 ahead of those who aren't even in the game!

FAKES

"It's Just Business."

Words that cowards hide behind to sidestep decent human behaviour.

This section is about being authentic. Don't wear a mask. Corporate behaviour is the death of happiness. What's the point in running a business for yourself if you still have to *'play the game'* with people?

Most people in this scenario don't even realise that's what they've become. They get indoctrinated into a culture, and it happens in most office spaces. There are different niches depending on the industry, but the principals are the same. Pretending to like people, instead of facing problems head on. It's really false and it's all gamesmanship ...and yet it's treated like a virtue. Employees get indoctrinated into becoming some cowardly shitbag, which helps them climb that greasy company pole.

You spot it in lots of different ways, and it can get old very quickly:

- They might try and slither out of paying for something.
- They might overly complain about something innocuous in order to get a discount or to find an excuse to drop you.
- They might be overly nice to your face – you've conducted yourself the same way since the relationship started but they suddenly blow up, usually through a cowardly, sassy email - instead of just admitting that they didn't have the balls to approach you about it in the first place.

These people actually unwittingly take their corporate attitudes into their personal life as well - then everything just becomes chess. You know those people that say: *"oh, it's just the analyst in me"* - shut the fuck up!

My advice as a business owner would be: Deal with problems up front, be honest, genuine and true. It might make you lose out in the short term, but at least you won't be a fake robot. Once you establish yourself a little more it won't stop you from getting results. Your great work will be more important to them.

For example, I used to wear a suit to meetings because I thought that impression is what mattered to people. I'd do the dance until I realised it was actually the quality of my work that mattered, so now I wear anything from Converse to Led Zeppelin t-shirts at meetings.

Beware of window dressing: Those that talk a good game. I don't do presentations to win work. I go in, listen intently and tell the client what they need to do. People appreciate it. No fancy consultations, presentations or proposals, tender processes, doing the corporate dance for someone.

You didn't get into business to kiss someone's ass - you could have a regular job and a boss for that. Your work, your product, your service and your results should speak for themselves.

Never trust anyone implicitly. Don't be a victim. Even the most seemingly respectful person you know can turn on you at a moment's notice – especially when money is involved.

A mentor once told me I was too soft for business, and at the time he was right. I presumed that everyone would have my best interests at heart, as that should be the easiest way for everyone to prosper. This is not the case. Of course, you must trust and build genuine friendships but as I've said before:

Never need something so much that you can't walk away.

Don't do business with fakes, corporate gimps and posers. Life is too short.

BAD CLIENTS

I'm unsure if this is supposed to be a touchy subject, as it's rarely covered in books. Also, as with everything in this book it'll vary from industry to industry, location to location, person to person - but the only people I'm offending in covering it are these kinds of bad clients, and who wants to be friendly with those people anyway?

Myself and my peers talk about this regularly and have done since we all started in business, offering each other support. So much so that to not touch on such an important subject here would be cowardly, because it will come up plenty on your business journey.

You need to know what to avoid and to understand that when someone's making you feel like shit and keeping you awake - it's not all in your head and it's not necessarily your fault.

Much like in the service industry where people believe because they are paying money they can stop treating others like human beings – you can find the same in business. Customers that expect you to roll over, tolerate their tantrums and shitty behaviour need to learn quickly that you are not a clerk in a 1980's department store – the customer is not always right, and will be told when they're being a dick.

You are not a punch bag for someone to inflict their inadequacies or insecurities on.

Here are some examples of bad clients:

UNREALISTIC DEADLINES

Customers that have probably procrastinated over getting a particular thing sorted but have left it late and want to dump that incompetence on to you. They will say they need something then say *"…and I need it by tomorrow / Friday / next week"*, something that is clearly unreasonable, but expect it to be done because they are paying and assume you have no other clients and are just sitting around, waiting for them to call.

FAKE DEADLINES

More of a compliance test borne out of some strange insecurity. Demanding or whining about getting something quickly and then, when you turn it around quickly for them, on time, they then do nothing with it for ages. All of this *'hurry up'* mentality, you move heaven and earth to get it done and they don't even action it for weeks or months later – and sometimes don't even use it at all!

BOUNDARY TESTERS

Don't tolerate customers that test your boundaries. It gets very tedious and it's often very underhand and Machiavellian – the polite advice is to rise above it, but the truth is you need to be better at it than them until you can fire them, because if you call them out on it they'll just deny it. Don't be afraid to walk away from a client, refund a client, phase out a client that's playing the game and not being authentic with you.

CALLS OUT OF HOURS

Usually comes from the same clients above. They do not respect your time or your space. Calls at 9pm at night, texts at 11pm, again for nothing urgent that couldn't wait until the following day.

PROJECTORS

Clients that deflect blame from themselves. They've not done the required work, they don't take your advice or instruction, they spend their money poorly and somehow it is your fault for time delays and poor results.

CHEAPSKATES

Some people know the cost of everything and the value of nothing. An important lesson is to deal with people **who only deal in the value of other people**, not on price.

You will find certain potential clients that only deal on price, they want a bargain, they want to squeeze every penny from you. They can even lie about the results you get or about how good your product is - just to make you work harder for them or give them something cheaper. I've had clients lie about how many leads they've had, not paying attention to the fact I could track them all!

You could be a Third Reich activist, but because you're cheaper they'd still pick you over someone else with integrity. The type that would complain about anything in a restaurant if it meant getting a discount or a freebie. It's making my skin crawl thinking about it as I type.

Interestingly, this is also a trait of those whose own products are typically more expensive than the industry average:

"I have high-end prices in my particular industry, but I somehow want to pay low-end rates for every business service I use."

Stick to those who care about people. If you have integrity, they'll stay with you through anything.

If you're giving something away for free in your business in order for a potential buyer to sample your quality as proof before pulling the trigger, that's fine – free because that person just wants something for free is the wrong kind of free and the wrong kind of marketing. They're cheap, they don't know the value of anything, and you shouldn't be competing on price.

UNREALISTIC EXPECTATIONS

Usually the same client as above. Be sure to manage expectations at the start, in the form of a digital footprint (email, text, instant message etc.) for reference, because no matter how much you explain the length of time things take, the results they can expect in relation to what they are spending and so on – they will be back on the phone demanding industry defying results a week later.

The clients that pay you the most tend to give you the least amount of issue in this area. They also tend to be the most successful in business. Funny that.

VISION LACKERS

Some clients lack the basic vision for what you provide. Particularly if your business is a service, rather than a product:

"I paid X for something therefore I should literally see something in front of me that correlates to that".

No matter how much you break down what you do for them - they just don't get it. They have random tantrums, act petulantly and irrationally but then when you try to explain what you are doing and why it's going to work in the simplest way possible, they still just glaze over when they should be listening.

GROUP OPINIONS

"This looks great, but I want to send this out to all of the team for feedback."

Too many cooks spoil the broth. Group opinions are the worst. Particularly when the people being asked aren't qualified to answer, or when there's a paid expert involved (usually you) and your **expertise** are overruled by **opinion**.

All too often these opinions come from someone desperate to justify their role in the company, or something mental like their wife, husband …or 8-year-old nephew (an actual one I had for a B2B website).

We're talking about coming to a decision an expert has been paid to make on a business that the customer has built from scratch based on *'keeping the peace'* and *'so not to offend by going against their employees or partners' opinion'*. Crazy.

"OHHH SHINY!"

The *"oh shiny"* that wants to try something new every 5 minutes, panicking they're missing out. Or the ones that want a fancy shiny product or service rather than one that actually works because it looks flash, or they can brag about what it cost them to their buddies on the golf course.

*"Videos are the big thing now, **so we need to be doing videos!**"*

…with no conversation, plan or understanding of how best to utilise it. Yes, you must explore different avenues to find out what works, but being reactive and half-arsing everything - dropping what you were focusing on previously in place of the next fad is not good.

They are either perpetual losers with rubbish businesses because they never focus and grow one thing into something excellent or they might be clients that have *'made it'* but waste the money they've worked hard to earn on vanity projects. They might make you lots of money but there's no soul in it. They'll drop work you've spent a lot of time on like a hot potato for the next thing.

These are just some of the common examples of bad clients, but every single one of these instances can be quashed by making sure you get on your hind legs. Don't be afraid to speak up. You are the one being paid so make it known. Explain why opinions are shit, they will respect you for it. Most importantly – don't be afraid to fire the client. Don't be afraid to walk away at the start if you get the sense potential clients are going to be more trouble than they're worth.

Nothing is worth the sacrifice of your mental health, your sleep at night or

your integrity.

You will learn that the business landscape is full of fantastic people. Some are superstars who have an aptitude for it and just *'get'* what you're trying to do for them. They let you - the expert, get on with things. Some are wonderfully nice people that are passionate about the service they provide that just need a little extra coaching through what you're doing in order to understand.

Some people are just idiots.

Thankfully I've learned not to work with idiots.

Like any group of people since the dawn of time there will always be morons and exploitative people. It's a hard thing to deal with if you're naturally a nice person, because **of course** you want everything to be right in their world and yours, but you **must** build resilience and cultivate your mental muscle.

The lies people tell themselves about the way they behave, for example, not paying you, stems from the same principal discussed in the first section. It's the mental gymnastics people go through to justify, well, just about anything.

That's why it's important to have a digital footprint for everything that you do. You must be able to evidence everything. Some people will do anything to get out of paying you. If you're unable to suss them out early, then you **must** keep that digital footprint.

Do not deal with people who you suspect aren't honourable.

Understand that it's not a case of *"how do they sleep at night!"* - they sleep just fine; their conscience is clear through the myriad of mental gymnastics they've done to justify their behaviour. They may try and gaslight you, or try to convince you that it's your issue, so it's important to have that digital footprint to:

- Stop you second guessing yourself.

- Supply evidence when you go through the appropriate channels to, say, recover your money.

- See things from both sides. If you look back over the digital footprint and realise you could have done better or more, then you must take accountability and own it.

Avoid making things public. These people have no shame, and remember - they've convinced themselves that they've done no wrong, so you won't shame them into it.

If you look at the facts and you've done the right thing, then you may have to accept that the other person is an idiot and not worth losing sleep over. Business owners aren't smarter because they're business owners.

Remember, if you're ever in doubt at any point, just re-read this section.

Also, accept the fact that not everyone wants to be your customer. You might be the problem – meaning you don't click with someone, your face doesn't fit or they just like someone else better. You might have the perfect solution for them, but they go with someone else. Not because that person was cheaper or flashier – but it could be anything from the other companies' guy supporting the same sports team as them …to them just not liking or clicking with you.

Those aren't *'Bad Clients'* – those are human beings with preference. Make sure your ego knows the difference.

GETTING MORE TECHNICAL & SOME BUSINESS THEORY

My best business decision to date:

Hiring a VA

What is a VA? VA stands for *"Virtual Assistant"* and the clue is in the name. Everything you need from an office assistant but on the end of the phone, email or chat box; instead of physically being there.

"That's not as good then, is it?"

To hire an assistant, you would need to ensure you had 40 hours of work a week, every week for that assistant to do. Maybe 16 hours if it's part time, but that's it, that set amount every single week:

"But I need you for more than 16 hours this week, we've just won a big contract!"

"Sorry boss, not my problem."

So, then you need to interview, employ and train another member of staff. In hope that:

- Their standard of work is at least as good.
- The same workload continues to flow in indefinitely.

Or the opposite…

"We lost that contract, so I don't need you for that many hours this week. I won't be paying you your regular amount."

(Probably don't need a hypothetical quote to know that the response to that would be)

It's a fantastic foundation for those that do all of their own work, all of their own tasks both large and small. You can hand over whatever volume of work you're comfortable with and scale it as:

- You get more comfortable with the right VA.
- Your business grows.

I don't have the desire to be entirely hands off. As much as I champion VA's here - being completely passive would be disingenuous to my clients, as everything about my business is them getting my knowledge and expertise …plus it would give me untold anxiety as a known control freak to release control completely!

What **can** you let go of? The boring answer is, it'll vary vastly from business to business, person to person. Something light for me, like answering emails, isn't a big workload (and I want my clients to know they get me personally when they message). This might be an absolute nightmare for you that, given the sheer volume, completely consumes your day. Maybe you're out in the field working and worry about missing any urgent emails …and so on.

However, some of my client work, while taking my expertise to create and build into a success can occasionally be monotonous and time consuming to implement certain parts. These are the areas in which my VA has become invaluable.

Anything that requires a few steps to learn; I explain in an email, over the phone or do a screencast (record what I'm doing on my computer screen) and send it over.

It's important to note: I've never been able to release control over my work in any form, to the point now, looking back, it was ridiculous. Now, anything I do that fits the criteria of:

- Not requiring my personal skill.
- I don't enjoy.

…gets handed over.

I just want to do my best work, in the order that I should be doing it, to the deadline that's set. I don't want to organise this. It's another one of those things that fits the above criteria:

- Finish something? Let my VA know.
- New client or job? Let my VA know.
- Sudden change of plan? Let my VA know.

Everything made into a regularly updated, streamlined list. I pick what I want to get done that day, get my head down and do it.

Other benefits? I've heard people occasionally talk about the *'adjustment period'* of using a VA. I have to say it was completely seamless for me and just all round common sense.

"Am I doing this right?"

"What about this particular situation?"

Questions that are asked just once. Then it's done forever!

A small business owner or freelancer like a VA is typically more vested in the work they do, as it means repeat business. Their business grows through good work and doing anything bad would reflect on themselves (and their reviews, if they use freelance websites to win work).

You're also giving a fellow small business owner or freelancer work, which helps them grow in the same way you do. Your growth often means growth for them!

Your choice of VA is vast in terms of price and location, if they are part of an agency or a freelancer. As covered previously, a lot of business owners obsess about getting the cheapest possible deal on any service they use.

These people know the cost of everything, but the value of nothing.

I use someone local and self-employed. I find they not only speak and type fluent English, they also get cultural nuances (not just Western or UK, but Scottish and Glasgow) and this helps greatly when understanding mind-sets and approaching situations.

…and I did it for **me**. I've not increased my prices as a result of having a VA. It's not a charge I pass on to my clients. I did it for me in order to be free to provide a better service and focus on the things I'm good at.

Because I can do more of this, I get better results, feel better, enjoy my business more and never feel intimidated with workload.

I can also take on bigger, more laborious projects that I would normally leave to marketing agencies with an abundance of staff. I would typically avoid these kind of jobs as it includes more repetitive tasks like data entry rather than just my specialist expertise. I'd be unable to trust outsourcing on such short notice and high stakes, but this takes the risk away because I know the quality of my VA.

If you have certain workloads you don't want to do, that eat up your time and can be outsourced with no drop in quality, why wouldn't you outsource? It frees you to do more of your best work and allows you to take on more business.

What's the point of me telling you about my awesome VA? Because as I explained earlier in this section it's important to play to your strengths and involve others in supporting your weaknesses.

Where are you weak in your business? If you can train yourself and motivate yourself to do it, then get on with it! Otherwise pay someone to plug that gap as soon as you can.

Employment is a minefield, there are better people than me to advise you if you need to go down that route, but don't expect employees to care as much about your business as you.

This means they won't work or sell as hard as you. They only care about themselves, and that's ok.

If the person at your desk handling your calls isn't on commission, then they won't care if they're not converting the sales calls, as long as they're getting paid.

They only time they'll care is when it's too late and you can't afford to pay them at all!

The difference between entrepreneurs and companies is companies typically need to fill a specific role, and they will almost always hire down. An entrepreneur understands that roles are not rigid - there are a myriad of instances and eventualities that come up in business. You are not there to press the button you've been trained to press all day, you are there to solve problems and be flexible. Not in a *"Work multiple roles so we can underpay you and hire less people"* way, but someone dynamic who can adapt to situations, solve problems and be a true asset.

A good entrepreneur doesn't fear hiring up. They welcome someone smarter than them in any instances they can get, as they know their business will improve drastically. They leave their ego at the door and allow the employee to flourish.

PAYING FOR THE RESULT

Understand that in business you are paying for the result: That is why the price of a product for *'hours worked'* is less important and why you should be focusing on the end result.

I was having a conversation with a friend a while back about something I was thinking about purchasing…

Rock Singing Lessons!

Now, the reason for having these lessons is another story entirely, but the conversation went something like this:

I'm thinking of purchasing these rock singing lessons. The guy is an amazing teacher. His video course guarantees that by the end you can competently sing like a rock and roll front man in many different styles.

"How much does it cost?"

The full, most expensive course is around $250.

"Wow, that's expensive! How many hours of teaching is that?"

Is $250 expensive for my end result? Putting aside the discipline I'll need to start and finish the course and the time I need to set aside (I'd need to do all that anyway), both of which have nothing to do with the product's effectiveness – $250 to be properly trained to sing like a rock star, a skill I've always wanted to have? It's not expensive at all.

It's actually why online information products are making more millionaires these days than any other industry, but that's a story for the next section.

Years in marketing has taught me to focus on the result. It's also what you should be focusing on. It's not about thinking you're too expensive for the number of hours you put in or how complicated your product is, it's:

Is the cost worth the end result?

There's a good anecdote about a graphic designer. The old story goes that a big executive asks the graphic designer to design a mock-up of a new product, logo or whatever. The designer comes back in half an hour with exactly what the executive is looking for. It looks amazing. The executive says:

"There's no way I'm paying X for that! I know it only took you 30 minutes!"

The designer goes on to explain how it actually took years of study, practice and dedication to their craft to be able to do it in 30 minutes.

Why should the executive care anyway? He got exactly what he wanted. Would it have made him feel better if the designer left and took a week to come back with that mock-up? He's focusing on the wrong thing.

A few years ago, my friend wanted a redesign of his website. We were sitting, about to watch a film and I said:

"I bet you a pizza I can completely redesign your website with dummy content before this film finishes."

He took the bet and I built the new website, with a modern design, parallax, fully responsive (desktop, laptop, tablet and phone optimized), testimonials, services, portfolio, all in a Content Management System (CMS) allowing him to add all his content and update it himself, built in analytics and SEO. All in less than 90 minutes while I was half watching the film!*

So not only did it cost him the redesign, but a pizza too! Don't underestimate someone dedicated to their crafts ability to work extremely fast and efficiently – I've built hundreds of websites.

It's important to note that admittedly less than 1% of websites are completed this quickly. I had the benefit of my friend sitting next to me and okaying every stage of the process and I also had full creative license to 'freestyle'.

The less time the better!

So, back to the singing lessons and the graphic designer's timescale: Should the graphic designer leave and bring the mock-up back after a week to make it **seem** like they spent more time on it? Should the singing lessons be as many hours as the instructor can pad it out to make it seem like more value?

Of course not!

More value shouldn't be a longer time spent – there's more value in being able to do it quicker! (providing it can genuinely be done without sacrificing quality).

What's better?

"$250 gets you over 30 hours of rock singing lesson content!"

or

"$250 to teach you how to sing like a rock star by a professional coach in less than 10 hours!"

The person who wants to buy the second one is the one I'd rather sell to.

"Simplicity is the ultimate sophistication."
- Leonardo Da Vinci

Remember, customers and clients should be paying for **the result**.

The size of the product or a shorter than expected timescale should not matter. Some get caught up in *"I'm not paying X for something that size or for that amount of time"* – focus on the result. You're paying for the result.

- Is $250 worth learning to sing properly? Of course it is.
- A life coach is charging you £1,000 to guarantee they cure your severe anxiety. You want to travel the world. Is it expensive? No.
- A marketing company is charging you £10,000 a month. They guarantee to get you £100,000 more in business a month. Is that expensive? No.

So, the next time you're doing market research about your pricing, be careful who you take advice from. Before you hesitate to send that invoice because you feel you aren't worth it due to the time taken, remember:

The loudest voices often come from the cheapest seats.

Be brave about your pricing. Dare to have a great product that doesn't need to compete on price and a race to the bottom. Be better than *'good enough'* and the minimum bar of entry.

Always look for better clients. Not in terms of price but in terms of ambition. If they are the ones wanting *'good enough'* then they can open their front door, throw a rock and hit 10 of your competitors. Be better and get clients that will pay for the result.

UNDERSTANDING TARGETS

Your targets cannot be *'get more business this year'*. It needs to be something like:

"I want to make 50k this year."

or

"I want to grow the business by 20%."

Set actual, measurable milestones. If you do anything else, then it's subjective or ambiguous and you quite simply won't follow through.

Have you woken up without any goals for the day? In that case, you haven't really woken up – you're **sleepwalking!**

One of the most important things to learn in any business, regardless of if you're just starting out or if you're a 50-year veteran is:

Goal setting.

Not in your head but **written down!**

It's the sure-fire way to make sure you're on the right track. A healthy combination of your business commitments and working **on your business** is an absolute must. Far too often business owners get drawn into the day to day slog, going through the motions of client work with no direction or long-term goal.

Growth doesn't just need to be business size or earnings related:

- Do you want more free time?
- Do you want to delegate things better?
- Maybe you have an exit strategy?

Get Unemployed

The absolute best thing you can do is to get a coach to combat the fog. You want someone to hold you accountable for your actions, someone that forces you to take a step back and evaluate where you're going and what you want to ultimately achieve.

The next best thing is to write it down (something any good coach will tell you to do anyway):

1. Start by taking that step back I mentioned. Find somewhere quiet without distraction, grab a pen and paper and really think about your business. What you think of it at the moment and where you want it to be. It's not a one-minute job either. Often what you initially think you want isn't actually the case. That's because you haven't taken the quiet time out before (or in a long time) to really delve deep into it. Write down everything that's in your head.

2. Once you're there it becomes about the goal setting. How much time you delegate to it can be at the mercy of how busy and involved you are in your day to day running. I personally used to have around a 50/50 split between working **on** my business and working **in** my business before things got crazy. I love what I do, but I've got to keep on track with where things are going if I want to grow the right way. Set your goals out clearly.

3. Now that you've set your goals you need to break it down and decide how much you can do each week. You have to be realistic based on your commitments detailed in the previous step, but you also need to be aggressive in your commitment or it won't get done. I recommend **3 to 5** broken down tasks per week.

4. Take action every week! (the hardest part).

Think About It…

Even just 3 tasks per week is around 150 tasks per year. **One hundred and fifty tasks ahead on moving your business forward** instead of:

"I keep meaning to do something about that, but I keep putting it off."

Don't put it off any longer and start setting goals!

Take the time, not instead of work, not instead of family time… but instead of TV time, instead of Facebook surfing time to work on the things that'll get you where you want to be.

Say you normally spend **3 hours a day** chill time (and that's being conservative), that's **1000 hours a year**. Spend **100 of that** a year on this **(2 hours PER WEEK**

98

total) and completely change your business.

10% of your chill time per week to get you where you want to be, to chase the goals and tasks you keep putting off.

Force yourself to take the action and don't let it become another year of:

"I should be doing this!"

...then prioritising something else and not getting any further forward ...or start, only to tail off after a few weeks. Either do it yourself or pay someone properly to handle it for you and give you accountability.

I also recommend putting your thoughts down on paper as well as your tasks. Typing them out, getting them out of your head and stored somewhere that you can revisit without having to use your memory all the time helps kill anxiety. It stopped me tying myself in knots and feeling like I was spinning plates all the time. It wasn't that I was overwhelmed by the work – I was overwhelmed trying to store it in my head and remember everything all at once. So simple, but so effective. It also gave me the framework of a book...

MASTERMIND GROUPS

I don't miss working with colleagues. In fact, it's one of the reasons I wanted to work for myself, mostly because you can't choose them.

A Mastermind Group is an organised collection of people, typically business owners and typically in the same or similar industry to yourself that meet up at time intervals agreed to talk about business, talk about goals and get support on achieving those goals.

With a Mastermind Group (and more broadly business in general) you only have to work with who you like.

Imagine an opportunity to meet with those who you admire, who inspire you and have the same mindset only.

As time passes and bonds form, you find a very special group of people you trust that also help you see things differently. You might have the same goals, or they might be completely different - but you're all there to support each other and hold each other accountable in getting there.

You can bounce ideas off each other, get support regarding difficult clients or perhaps get an introduction into a potential company or client that someone else in the group knows! Maybe they might know someone in a particular demographic or industry you're looking for? It doesn't need to be just business either, it can help all aspects of your life!

As I touched on briefly in the previous section, I have friends I originally met through business where we all help support each other with our goals.

It started as a mastermind group, but it became a bunch of guys going out for food and beers.

7 years after it started we still meet up at least once a month, without fail. All 5 of

us have reasonably diverse skillsets and can often lend a hand or lean on each other for specific advice where our fields cross paths.

I've seen structured masterminds where there are agendas and *"who's turn to talk"*, but to me that's just like being in some cold corporate work environment where everyone was polite to each other, chose their words carefully and were out for nothing other than growing their own business. That might be what suits you, and it's arguably easier to set up because everything can be structured down to the letter.

For your mastermind, pick a time and a place to suit everyone - even online if you prefer (or in order to break down distance and time barriers). I find these things begin better as a loose outline and then you can let them flow into their natural rhythm.

The only rule I advise is being strict on who you let in.

If you start with a really good core group then they'll *'get it'* and only invite those who are truly of the same mindset, who won't poison the group with bitching, petty drama, poor advice, have a chip on their shoulder or talk down to members. This should go without saying, but it can be more difficult in practice.

It's also a good idea to keep the conversation going out-with the meeting dates. Have a group chat on WhatsApp or Facebook Messenger for example to maintain the connection and support, and to keep those that maybe couldn't make one of the meetings up to date.

Our group even bought PlayStations to hang out and play online! None of us are exactly hard-core gamers, we're pretty shit at it, but we all get online at some point every week and everyone actually makes time for it!

Make the effort and find the time for the right people.

As I've mentioned, it's important to talk for a number of reasons:

- The group might be able to help in a practical sense or give advice.

- They might know someone that can help or put you in touch with the connections you're looking for.

- Sometimes, and most importantly – they can get you out of your head simply by having you air your thoughts and think out loud. Without even receiving any advice, this is a massive help!

The power of group knowledge and support with the right people can grow you rapidly. You might also want to do some collaborations and cross promotion, but we'll talk about that in more detail in the next section!

The best bit about Mastermind Groups isn't about what you get out of it for your business – it's about what you get out of it for **you**. Helping others is even better than helping yourself and building relationships with likeminded people is good for the soul, in a way that can't be measured in money. It's a different kind of success.

*"...it's telling people your **Wishes** and **Obstacles**. Here is what I want and here is why I cannot have it. It echoes... in no magical, new age way - it echoes in practical ways. You have to let people help you. We depend on other people's dreams coming true."*
- Barbara Sher

RUNNING A SUCCESSFUL BUSINESS

As we've covered, business is about:

- The right offer, to the right people, at the right time.

- It's about delivering value and doing whatever it legitimately takes to get those first clients in, packaged in an offer that can't be refused.

- It's about being willing to adapt and adjust to what the market wants – a product or service that meets a genuine demand.

- It's about becoming an irreplaceable asset.

- It's about automated processes and hiring those that will support your failings or weaknesses to bypass roadblocks, allowing you to focus on what you're good at and scale your business.

- It's about setting real goals and persisting until you make those goals a reality.

- It's about involving others that you can trust on your business journey to help and reward you in many different ways.

So, if you understand this – then avoid vanity. Don't become obsessed with website views, social media likes and so on, because you start using that as the measure of what you're worth, or your businesses worth. This is a complete distraction. What matters is traffic developing into paying clients.

Find out what works and do more of that.

Website views mean nothing if nobody is buying - but more on this in the next section.

Unless you're starting a YouTube channel that's purely monetised by ads based on user volume then fuck views, likes and subscribers - you're running a business, not a popularity contest.

Supply a product or service that your customers are actually asking for. A smaller group of customers that truly get your niche are infinitely more valuable than an ego driven number – there are no exceptions.

Once you're over the hurdle of finding the right product or service and are now winning clients – what's next?

Winning new customers from a cold audience is the hardest gig of all. What you should be thinking about moving forward is how to get **existing** customers to:

- Spend more.
- Buy again.
- …and encourage their friends and family to buy also.

More on the nuts and bolts of how to do all of that in the next section.

Once you've got processes in place to cover existing customers then you want to move into **leverage**. Leverage is not working one-to-one with clients, and there are varying degrees of how it's done.

A good example would a personal trainer. No matter how good a trainer you are, if you only do one-to-one coaching then there's a cap on how much you can earn, even if you have a high hourly rate, you're at the mercy of how many hours there are in a day.

So how can this be leveraged? As I say - there are degrees of leverage. A simple starting point would be group classes. Why teach one person at a time when you can have multiple clients in a class? Let's say you're really good and you typically charge £60 per hour for one-to-one coaching. If you charge 8 people £20 per hour for a group class, you're now making £160 per hour!

This is not just making the service more affordable to more people; you're building a community. You create a bigger reach, as more customers talk to more people like friends and family about your service. It also minimises loss, as losing a one-to-one coaching client can mean a big drop in revenue for that week, month or year, but if one of your group members misses a week or stops coming entirely it's not as big a deal.

The next stage in leverage is no longer trading time for money at all – it's about being truly passive. You are truly passive once you are creating products that you can sell to infinity for no extra work. Examples of this would be writing a book or designing an online course.

Every time someone buys your book – do you need to write each one out from scratch?

Of course not.

You write the book once and have it published, either as a physical product, on kindle or an eBook and then it doesn't matter how many you sell – the workload was the same. When someone buys it – the order is automatically filled and you're literally making money while you sleep.

Being paid while you sleep and poop!

You now have an asset that you can sell many times over for however many years that the book is relevant – so potentially to infinity.

If you're currently running your business in such a way that it **needs** you, then what happens if you get injured or are faced with a debilitating illness? What does that mean for your business and your responsibilities when you can no longer trade your time for money? It's not a nice conversation to have with yourself, particularly if you're young, and it's likely the last thing on your mind – but life can strike at any time. Passive income allows you to continue earning in spite of sticky life situations.

Designing an online course can have the same principal as a book – a one-time fee in exchange for a collection of videos or an eBook.

Sticking with the personal training example: Instead of group coaching you could film yourself presenting the class and then sell the course to as many people online that wish to buy – and you only filmed it once!

You have that asset forever.

Not only that, but online courses can also be subscription based. Monthly fees, yearly fees and so on. You can continue adding videos (or whatever your format is) encouraging your customers to continue paying a fee that is guaranteed passive income for you!

Remember in the first section I mentioned producers and consumers?

Producers that use leverage are those that have cracked the successful business code if there ever was one.

TO FINISH THIS SECTION

As I mentioned before, running a business **is** hard, but not in the ways you probably think.

Don't feel you need to get to where you want to be as fast as possible. Don't lose patience and feel like a failure. It all takes time and persistence. Don't sacrifice your mental health or your integrity getting there. Take the long road, it tastes better at the end – knowing the struggles you had and overcame. We shouldn't need instant gratification or feel insecure about not winning right away through fear of what others might think. Stay in the game.

Don't talk shit about the bad times, particularly when everything is going well, and you're suddenly blindsided with a setback. This humbles you, keeps you grounded and tests your mettle.

Stick at it and have persistence. You will do it.

At time of writing, the business world is going good, but it definitely wasn't during the recession when I started. Get in while it's the safest to do so and build the processes for when it's not.

When the next recession hits, is your business or your job bullet proof? When money's easy, everyone spends. What does that look like when they don't? Are your processes, your systems and so on air-tight? What about your leads - do you just rely on what comes in or do you have a tap that you can turn on when things go a bit sideways? What about your offering - is it recession proof? What makes you better than the next person, so when people can only afford to be picky - you come out on top? That can be anything from quality to price. Is your business (or you) being a little too lackadaisical in what you spent your profits on? All of a sudden, your earnings dry up and you're in a self-inflicted financial problem that you in turn blame on the collapse.

I'm not greedy and I have low overheads. I get good results for my clients because

106

I'm up to date with my industry, what's new and what's working – honing my craft. I'll always be in demand.

Can you say the same?

MARKETING

BEFORE WE BEGIN

Pay for your marketing or do your own. One or the other. You can't excuse your way out of this if you want more customers. You can't say:

*"I'm too busy **and** I can't afford it"*

If that's the case you're not charging enough, your times poorly spent or you're not being honest with yourself. It's usually the last one. If you really are too busy, flat out to the point you can't do your own marketing, then you must be making enough to pay for it. You can't have it both ways. If you want more business, you'll make it work – **no excuses**.

MARKETING THEORY

There's no doubt niching down in your business helps. The more specialised you can be with your service, the higher the fees you can charge and the more you will be in demand.

Take my own industry for example:

Person A says they are a Facebook Ad expert.

Person B says they are a Facebook Ad expert, specialising only for Personal Trainers.

It's not hard to see who a PT would prefer to spend their money with – even if Person B was a little more expensive.

The truth about marketing is - if you're good, the industry doesn't make much of a difference. The principals are pretty much universal. Get a strong background in a particular industry by taking time out to research, along with a lengthy conversation with the client, can have a good marketer confidently moving into any arena.

The *'specialist'* has usually just marketed themselves that way because they understand the human behaviour of being much more likely to pick Person B if they fit the criteria. They can charge more and that their processes are already streamlined for each client that comes on board – rather than providing a bespoke service to each differing client.

Even though niching down in both service and industry was the smartest move to make money, I never wanted to. I love learning new industries, applying my knowledge to different services and enjoy having a variety of different clients.

I basically learned to do everything in digital marketing because marketing that actually works is a cocktail of things. For example, I could have just specialised in Search Engine Optimisation (SEO) and carved myself out as an expert, only dealing in that medium. Each client that came to me would then pay for SEO, nothing else.

But sometimes SEO isn't the right medium for a business and sometimes you don't find this out until you've already started. So, you go down this route of spending money, only for it to bear no fruit. You've wasted your money (other than finding out SEO doesn't suit your model) and you need to look for a provider of something else.

As I say, what works is testing a cocktail of things and finding out what works best for your business. Of course, there's a degree of *'using the force'* and predicting what will work based on the clients' industry, the human behaviour of that industry and the types of audiences that are on each marketing platform – but you won't know for sure until you test.

That's why I felt I had to learn everything. I project manage and implement the entire online marketing of each client I work with. Not to mention, when you've been brought in to do one platform, you then need to liaise with your clients *'other-areas-of-marketing'* freelancers or agencies …or they don't have *'other-area-of-marketing'* people - so you need to become all of them to make sure the project gets implemented correctly.

I never rely on one source of marketing for clients when there are so many different avenues to explore:

- Technical aspects like business processes and sales funnels.
- Specialist work like copywriting; email marketing; social media advertising; SEO and PPC.
- Design work like websites; graphic design for logos; image manipulation; digital posters and fliers.

…and being a project manager for the whole thing.

The more I did this, the more I wanted to do it all. I wanted full control over the entire strategy and could implement it exactly as I envisioned.

That's why I've never niched down in any one marketing discipline:

You don't know what works best until you try everything – then you do more of what works!

But for other types of business, finding a niche in both skillset and market is something you should seriously consider. The human behaviour works favourably on it.

My lack of niching down is now your gain – because I'm going to write about the different online marketing avenues later in this section!

Take it from my experience in working with 100's of marketing strategies - fancy rarely works.

Marketing is about finding out what works and doing more of that.

Leave your ego at the door. Having a fancy website, branding, app or cheesy explainer video isn't important. Stop throwing money at ego-driven, dick-waving snobbery. Looking fancy isn't important - what works is what's important.

We're still predominantly using our *'Chimp Brain'*.

Our world today has moved on. We've become far more advanced from when we were hiding in caves. We've streamlined and refined ourselves. We have socially acceptable behaviour now and standards of how you conduct yourself in society need to be met.

…but biologically - we haven't moved as fast. The biggest parts of our minds are still primal:

- Climbing trees.
- Foraging for nuts and berries.
- Hunting deer and fish.
- Looking for acceptance from our peers.
- Enjoying song and cheer around the camp fire.
- Sleeping in.
- Finding someone who will mate with us.

You need to market to this brain. The real brain that's not built for 9 to 5.

The façade people walk around with, the mask they wear, the way they behave is social conditioning, not their true desires – this is evident in the real reasons people buy things:

We buy things with emotion and justify it with logic.

Think of the last reasonable purchase you made - chances are it was emotion disguised as logic. You tell yourself the reasons you bought it were rational to justify your real emotion governing it. In your marketing you must spend 95% of your copy, images and video stroking emotions as they are the real reason your customer will buy. The other 5% is giving them a list of logical reasons why they should buy so as to justify that decision to themselves and others.

It's subconscious, and we can't do much about it. That sucks for us as rational humans, but it's great for marketing! All the best marketing in the world exploits this crutch.

We rarely want or buy things that we really, truly need. Everything else is emotion.

So, what does marketing to emotions look like?

The image you portray – how you're seen with a particular product. Nobody will admit they want that Chanel handbag because they want others to envy them, they want others to respect them, they want others to think they are a high value person.

They tell themselves it's because the bag looks nice (actually meaning other people see that it looks nice) or that the bags are good quality (even though there are similar bags with the same quality leather with gold details that are less than a tenth of the price).

If you sell handbags, your job is to market to this. You wouldn't typically say in your copy:

"This bag will make your friends jealous!"

You can't outwardly say the real reasons because remember – they are trying to justify it with logic. You have to **convey** these things in your copy:

"This is the finest handbag money can buy."
"Those who buy this handbag understand what quality is."
"Be seen with this year's 'Must Have' accessory."

As I mentioned before, I've read so many books on Direct Response Copywriting over the last few years and designing your marketing strategy around this, along with a firm understanding of human behaviour is what's going to explode your success in just about any industry.

TRUST

Marketing is about trust.

This is more important than any funnel, more important than any advert, more important than any sales page.

Yes, your sales page weighs heavily on building trust, yes you can get sales from directing a good ad to a great sales page for a cold audience, but you probably don't have the 10k to sink into a single page for a master copywriter (yes, a real number), so what you should be doing is **building trust**.

Trust in business isn't what it typically means socially - it's about brand recognition, and not in the way agencies like to sell brand recognition:

"Hey, you just sank 10k into an ad campaign and got no leads, but don't worry you got something you can't buy - brand recognition!"

No.

By trust I mean others seeing you walk the walk, by seeing you produce results for other people they know or at least putting names to case studies and testimonials you show them. This is why reviews on your website, your Google listing and your social media is essential (along with your search engine rankings, but we'll get to that later).

You cannot sell without trust. Selling something to someone that hasn't heard of you or your product or service on the spot, without being literally face to face with them **is hard!**

It's much better to be actually good at what you do and proving it with real life examples. The only thing better than showing those real-life examples is one of those real-life examples telling someone else (which is what my own business model is based on).

By brand recognition I mean in terms of the *'Touch Principal'* (which I'll explain in more depth shortly) and building trust and familiarity that way. You build it up to the point where people are seeing you regularly from multiple angles, multiple times, gathering momentum:

- They keep seeing your Facebook ads.
- Your Retargeting ads following them round the web.
- You're inside their email inboxes.
- You're coming up on web searches they perform.
- Their friends are leaving reviews on your social media and Google.

What happens after building that momentum and brand is amazing - people just start buying. There comes a tipping point where people have seen enough to be comfortable buying – then it's your job to build on that and make the snowball bigger.

AUTHORITY

Building a brand is important because that also builds authority. When you have authority – you can sell anything. What does authority look like? Search for an item on Google and I guarantee if Amazon stock the item it'll be there in the first few results, very often ahead of industry specific results that relate to the product.

Amazon has built it's brand up to have such an authority that no matter what the product is – Google trusts them to showcase, sell and deliver that product well – even though Amazon isn't specific to that product.

Building authority is how Amazon's Jeff Bezos is now the richest man in the world.

…but you can't afford to run at a loss for 8 years like they did. So how do you build authority for your business or position yourself as a thought leader in your industry?

You can post on social media, blog, write books, record videos, join groups. Talk about your industry, encourage conversation in your space. Either do it personally and start by answering questions wherever your potential clients are hanging out or communicating, or make sure the content on your company website is educational and genuinely engaging. You need to get your legitimate and glowing case studies in front of people. Not just:

"Hi, my name is Bob and I sell insurance."

Well, good for you, Bob.

When you have authority, your reputation proceeds you. You should never have to be pushy in sales. Your reputation, having your own high value and being able to walk away are also key to sales - not your *'sales patter'*. You must relax, go with the flow and be ready to genuinely help the customer if you can. Listen and table a solution if you genuinely have one. People smell your desperation and your salesy attitude. Hard sales should only be reserved for sales pages, which we'll talk about later – every other conversation with a potential customer or client should be like smoking a cigar on a hammock; where the hard work is already done with your authority in your space.

BACK IT UP

Guy takes drag of cigarette…

Cough cough cough!!!

"…smoke cigarettes, they're amazing! They make your breath smell good too!"

What's wrong with the message? The actions (coughing in this instance) don't back up the claims about cigarettes being amazing. That statement is then followed up by another statement that everyone knows is a blatant lie.

Is every aspect of your business, from your interactions with your customer to your results, customer satisfaction and customer experience backing up what your marketing says? Do you claim to be the best but skimp on everything else? Do you make airy fairy bullshit claims that people know is either false or canned garbage?

I don't want McDonalds to claim they care about my health - they clearly don't. I want them to tell me their fries are delicious and accept the fact I won't be strong enough to eat clean all the time.

Exploit the chimp brain, but always be honest in your claims and back it up every day. Build trust and authority. Anyone can be a fraud – be the real deal, watch your business grow cleanly as a result and sleep easy at night.

POSITIONING YOURSELF AS PREMIUM

You get what you pay for, right? Well, most of the time. You'd like to think so anyway….

In an **ideal** market you would say that there's a direct correlation between the amount paid comparatively to the quality of the product. There are plenty of exceptions though. Selling a poor product for high ticket isn't being a brilliant businessperson, it's just misleading. Is your skill:

Providing a good service or product?

Or

Using marketing to *Dupe Suckers*?

I know where I'd rather be.

The Rational vs The Emotional mind:

People buy with their heart and justify it with their head.

Can you purchase equally as competent, sometimes better alternatives to the iPhone, iPad, iMac and MacBook? Yes. Usually cheaper, too. But some want the Apple anyway. Why? Because it's what they want.

You can't touch the value your heart places on it, but you understand how owning it makes you **feel**. It's also closely tied to your identity, about other people knowing what you buy.

Does your brand align with your customers in a deeper way than just what your product factually is? Are you cooler, are you more prestigious, are you more

118

environmentally conscious, do you produce your products out of love for the subject matter?

If this wasn't true, Apple would be a niche market, not a 40-billion-dollar annual profit company.

So how do they do it?

They know their customer.

Whatever you call it: Ideal Customer, Customer Avatar, Customer Profile – they understand their positioning. They know what their customers want; they give them what they want, and they don't compete on price because their customers aren't looking for the cheapest option.

So, are Apple *'Duping Suckers'*? No. Their products are still brilliant. That feeling they deliver through ownership is a benefit not a feature like processor speed, screen resolution or weight.

Imagine *'Features'* as your **business** and *'Benefits'* as your **clients**. Talk about your clients. People buy with their heart, not their head: Talk about the benefits, not the features. Of course you have to explain the features, the nuts and bolts of what you do help your client understand how you achieve the desired outcome and how they'll justify the purchase, but benefits will beat it every time when it comes to pulling the trigger.

What sounds better:

"I provide consulting for you and your business."

Or

"Never again should you feel stressed about the direction you and your business are travelling. I help you get better clients, more financial freedom and improved personal development while you focus on your business."

The first one is about the business, the second is about the benefit to the client. The bigger picture.

What does this have to do with positioning yourself as premium?

Those that provide a quality service also want quality and will pay the premium for the peace of mind that comes from that level of service.

Not only this, they will be better customers themselves. Not *'Problem Clients'* who bleed your resources dry and are the *'something for nothing'* type. In my business, people ask why customers are free to leave if they choose with no contracts. If your service is good, a quality customer will want to stay.

- First and foremost, you **must** provide a high-quality service, not a poor product disguised as premium product. A good customer will realise they're getting what they pay for. Make sure you provide this, and you will attract the right kind of clients.

- Secondly, understand your positioning. Know where you are in the market, give your clients what they want in the premium space and you won't have to worry about competing on price because you shouldn't be there in the first place.

- Lastly, focus on the customer (the benefits). Again, a good business recognises it's not about them and a good customer will recognise the quality of service and how that benefits them and their business.

Some businesses are so generic, so devoid of USP or higher standard that they will always be in the swamp where the cheap, needy, greedy clients reside.

NO KPI? WTF?!

This is something that comes up regularly when speaking to business owners and is big part of the Business Development side of my consulting.

A client of mine had two big agencies working for them and they were spending **a lot** on advertising across many different mediums (well into 6 figures annually).

When we all sat round the table in the big boardroom meeting, I asked:

"How much business are you getting as a result of said spend?"

…the room fell silent.

I won't go into more specifics than that because, as you'll discover, this thing goes far deeper than them.

I was casually telling this story, standing in a circle of pretty reasonably sized business owners and partners at a recent event. Again, those listening went silent:

"Yeah… I don't think we do that."

"We don't either."

"We should probably talk to you about that…"

So, what's KPI? Firstly, it's important to understand that nobody knows everything. Furthermore, nobody needs to. I don't need to know how to plan my investments, how to represent myself in court, how to install my boiler or fix my car. I have those who are specialists in their field to do it for me.

So, when I'm taking about this, it doesn't come from a patronising place, it comes from a *'whoever you're getting your advice from should really have this down already'* place. I don't want my mechanic to half-fix my car when I take it into the garage.

KPI = Key Performance Indicators.

This can vary for different companies. Anything from specific goals or targets down to simply measuring where your customers are coming from. We're focusing on the latter here because it's basic and you should get started as soon as you start a business, or right away if you're running one now.

Measuring is a little easier if you're a freelancer given your volume is relatively low. You can often tell where each client comes from on the fly. By the same token you should be assessing once a month where they come from. You'll find the 80/20 Rule comes into play pretty heavily here.

The 80/20 Rule (also known as the Pareto Principle) suggests 80% of your results come from 20% of your action.

So, although you may think all your tasks are equally important for the overall success of your business – a more important 20% of them are accounting for your 80% of your profits.

Not just profits – anything:

- 20% of your sales team produce 80% of your sales.
- 20% of your customers account for 80% of your revenue.
- 20% of your clients take up 80% of your time (not always in correlation to the one above, which is essential to fix).

…and so on.

So yes, 20% of your marketing efforts product 80% of your sales, customers, clients, revenue, whatever. 20% of your daily tasks help move your business forward by 80%. It's important you find out what these 20%'s are so you can double down on them, and preferably delegate the other 80%.

If you're reading that and feeling pedantic, no, it's not always exactly 80/20 but the principal that 1/5 of the work you do accounts for 4/5's of your success is important to keep in mind to make you work smart, not hard. Busy fools are a dime a dozen.

Getting lots of business from a particular source? Do more of that! (while still exploring new avenues of course, because you never know where your next 20% rule is going to come from).

Anyway, as I explained to the client in that boardroom:

"If you take nothing else from this meeting, and I don't care if it's literally a sheet of paper with a tally that your receptionist sits with - when someone comes off the street or you get a call from a

potential customer... **You ask and record how that person found your company!"**

...also, if you are currently running a business - begin some sort of campaign to find out where previous and existing clients came from to garner some historical data.

What's the point in spending all that money on advertising if you have no context for how well it's working? Spending 80% of your marketing budget on stuff that isn't yielding results? Spend more of it on the 20% that is! Again, make sure you've got a little left over to market to new platforms you haven't explored yet.

You should also be monitoring your **Churn**. As I mentioned previously, it's much easier to retain existing customers – not only to buy again but to spend more when they do. It can be more complex than this, but for the purpose of this section I want to talk about **Churn** in terms of clients dropping off to new clients coming in.

If your clients are on monthly retainers, when you're on-boarding more clients than those that leave – then your business grows. The measurement can become more complex if, say, 2 clients were to leave but 1 client comes in that pays the same amount as the 2 leaving combined. To keep it simple, where every client requires the same workload, then the 2 out, 1 in could be good for your business – same money, less workload. Perhaps you increased your prices and when historic clients that paid at your old rate dropped off, new clients at your new rate are coming in but are willing to pay more?

Do higher paying clients need more work, more investment or more responsibility, though?

What if you sell an online course or service with monthly subscription payments – are you bringing in more sales than those that cancel your monthly payment?

What if you run a gym? Are you bringing in more members than those that are cancelling?

Do you have a critical mass you can reach before you need to grow your premises, your team, your hosting, your software, your tech support or your outsourcing to service your customers effectively? Do you want to increase your prices in order to make more money or reduce workload? What about encouraging existing customers to spend more, or increase their retainer, or simply buy again? How will all of this effect your **Churn**? This is a lot easier than converting cold customers – so have you looked at this properly?

If you:

- Are spending thousands on advertising.
- Are getting enquiries.
- Don't regularly have a conversation with your marketing department or

agency about basic KPI.
- Aren't recording where your leads come from and have no context for spend.
- Aren't refining your spend to focus on what works (with some change left over to try other mediums).
- Aren't assessing your **Churn**.

Get it done...

...start...

...like yesterday!

CHANGES

The landscape changes so quickly, that's why the principals are more important than the actual tools you use to reach your customers. Once you understand the theory, the logic and buying motivations - you can apply them to anything.

When everyone was using print media to advertise nobody knew SEO would become huge, particularly when it became mainstream to business owners around 2010. Then a few years ago Facebook ads and Retargeting came along, and this has grown to become the sole solution for some businesses.

It would be easy to write an entire book on any of these mediums, but in truth anything new can come along to change the game, rendering the current methods obsolete. As I say, that's why it's far more important to understand the principals than any step by step instructions on how to use a particular marketing service - that's what free YouTube videos are for.

Not only do services come and go but they can also change their Terms of Service (TOS) at a moment's notice - disallowing anything they decide they don't want advertised any more.

Entire businesses can shut down because they have relied on the one marketing medium whose policy has changed and no longer allowing them to advertise in such a way that was the lifeblood of their leads.

A good example would be Teespring. There was a swell a few years ago of marketers selling customised t-shirts - and It worked **really** well:

- Pick the demographic you want to target, for example, fans of a particular band or sports team.
- Design a print for a t-shirt on Teespring relating to that band or team.
- Teespring does all the fulfilment, so you don't need to carry stock, just meet a minimum order number.
- Set up a sales page with a countdown timer in order to create demand and

scarcity.

- Send targeted Facebook ads only to Facebook users that Like the pages directly associated with the band or sports team.
- Get a bunch of orders.
- Repeat ad infinitum.

This worked so well in fact that many people left their jobs, business owners closed their doors or got rid of their clients to double down and focus solely on this venture, given how easy and lucrative it was.

Then Facebook changed their TOS and stopped allowing it.

Never allow another company to solely control your leads. No exceptions. Your entire livelihood based around one platform that you have no direct control over? Never.

I had a conversation with a friend about a Multi Level Marketing (MLM) business he was joining. He wasn't trying to sell to me, but he asked me to come along to a group presentation to get my opinion on it.

After watching the presentation, the only question I asked the presenter was about the TOS or whatever the guarantees were about the earnings, should the milestones be met. Not only now, but forever (people were doing quite well with this, quitting their jobs to pursue it full time with a view to have a lifetime of passive income).

He looked a little puzzled at what I was asking (presumably not in the generic book of canned questions they usually get) then said they all had a contract to protect them.

I told my friend in no uncertain terms to pursue this only in his spare time as an extra income, but not to quit his well-paid job – no matter how good the earnings seem to get.

I take no pleasure in saying that after only a few months the company changed their *'contract'*, as it wasn't worth the paper it was written on and changed the bonus structure to the point that the effort was barely worth many of its members even trying.

He never told me he remembered that was the only question I'd asked a few months back at the presentation. He was blinded by the potential earnings that were being sold to him.

Thankfully it happened way before he was looking to make the jump full time with it and kept his good job.

I'll be mentioning this again later but just to reiterate – do not go all in on a client or money stream that you **do not** control.

PAID ADVERTISING COSTS

Most business owners don't appreciate the amount you need to spend when you do paid advertising. So often I hear:

"I tried Facebook advertising, but it just didn't work out for me."

How much did you spend?

"Oh, I dunno, about £20-£40."

When you're testing at the very start, that's fine, maybe for a week at the absolute most. Your very first budget should be low while you get the data to then go ahead and improve the ad …but to write off the whole thing based on spending £40 is absolutely mental.

You have to break through and get enough traction, then build momentum, then your ad becomes a money-making asset. You can then spend more and more, knowing you'll be making much more back in sales.

Past customers have used me then tried to go it alone. They go right back to sporadically paying these pitiful amounts. You might as well go outside and take a Zippo to a couple of 20's.

The less you're willing to spend - the longer you need to wait.

You might get lucky and boost a post cheaply and get some quick wins for your crappy handmade campaign – there's always exceptions to any rule. Long term though you need to be spending decent money on a consistent basis to see results, learning and improving it, then you can scale it to where the sky can be the limit.

Everyone would own a 7-figure business if business owners applied the logic they have for Facebook ads and it actually worked. They think:

*"Well, I've spent this much, so that should translate into **this** amount of business."*

Business owners want to treat it like a money printer: *"I put X amount in, and I expect triple my spend back!"*. You have to build up to that. Social ads have made it much easier to get in front of your target market, but you still have to sell them - you still have to sell them while they're trying to chill and surf their feed. You have to actually have a good business that provides value, usually over and above your competition - and you need a killer offer. Not a tokenistic add-on because you're cheap - make it a no brainier for the viewer.

You then need to spend ad money building up the ad, having it bed-in, allowing Facebook's algorithm to send it to better people at better times. Facebook actively tells you to spend your money over a longer period, even though that doesn't benefit them financially. They know their bots needs to gather more data. Also remember to refine the ad yourself with the ad type, the imagery and the copy.

Social ads are the same as any other business principal - no one's going to just give you it by virtue of turning up; you need to work at it, spend money on it and persist. If it's not working? Chances are your business, your product or service and your offer aren't good enough - plus you've not given it enough time. If you want to throw your hands up in the air and have a tantrum about it, too bad - the market didn't want it. Do better.

Lazy people demand their marketing work immediately. They want a return on investment immediately:

"I paid £300 into Facebook ad campaigns and didn't get results! What a waste of money!"

If someone buys your service, how much is that client worth to you?

"On average, £1,000."

Jesus Christ, you think you've risked £300? You're still £700 shy of actually losing what it would take for 1 client to pay it back! You're not willing to risk, you want to play it safe and still demand it works for you right away!

You have to be willing to risk because that's where the reward is. £300 on marketing is nothing, you need data, you need to tweak your generic offer, the copy and images that portray that offer, you need to capture the viewers and retarget to them.

If I was to promote this book, spend less than the value of one book, then say it's a failure because I'm not getting the immediate return, then I'd have a pretty shit business.

If I was inclined, I'd happily spend thousands promoting it because of ...yes, the book sales, but even if I don't make thousands back in sales - which is likely given how inexpensive the book is - think of the reach. All those people that clicked:

- The exposure to new people.
- The contacts.
- The speaking gigs.
- The clients.

Think of those that did buy the book being re-marketed to bringing their lifetime value up. If I believe in my book, then I have to assume that people will like it and want to buy something else that I have.

If you're greedy, unwilling to lose or see the big picture then I've got bad news – paid marketing isn't for you, particularly if you've got a generic business with a generic offer and simply crossing your fingers that clients come in.

If you can't accept that you might not get a return on investment within months and don't understand that marketing is an ongoing improvement process until you're turning on new clients like a tap - then it's not for you.

…and if you're reading this and internally whining about how you can't afford to take that hit - then what are you unwilling to sacrifice?

"But I work 80 hours a week, have 10 kids and never treat myself!"

Whatever - do other avenues of marketing until you can afford the paid options.

I just read a case study of a 16-year-old on one of the Facebook groups I'm a member of. He spent $200 on Facebook ads, just to make $10 on his first sale, and he was ecstatic!

A 16-year-old understands the concept of marketing and ad spend - you have no excuse.

He now understands, through testing, what it was that got that first sale. Now all he has to do is refine that process, then scale it.

If you can't afford it just yet – that's absolutely fine. This isn't about belittling those that can't afford to do paid advertising. It's the half-assed, trying to do it yourself, wasting your money, then talking shit about whatever platform *"doesn't work"* that I won't listen to.

BEFORE YOU PAY

Before any paid marketing starts (or any marketing for that matter) you need to answer some questions:

- Who is your target market?
- Where do they hang out?
- What do they want? (Not what you want to sell them).
- What will they engage with?
- What are my competition doing **successfully**?
- What's working for me right now?

Decide either who you would like to sell to, or what customer profile fits your product best.

Are they online or offline? Are they on Facebook or LinkedIn? Do they attend certain events?

There should be testing but there should be no scattergun, spray and pray, hope-for-the-best, random spending. What solves their problems? What's the best medium? A face to face conversation? A video? Lots of text? Funny images?

I put successfully in bold above because in just about every industry there's a herd mentality. Do what everyone else does. Common sense would have you think everyone's doing it because it works. The sad truth is that; often everyone's doing it just because everyone's doing it.

Study, find out what your competitors are doing that **actually works**. It doesn't have to be local competition – search for information worldwide and adapt accordingly to your area.

Where are your customers coming from right now? Can you see a way in which doing the same thing but with the addition of paying for your advertising could help expand that reach?

Start with what you think will work.

Too many times I've wrongly predicted where most of the business is going to come from. No matter how much experience I get, no matter how successful the campaigns I run have been – there will be a business that comes along that a little test, where I'm just being sure to cover all bases, blows everything else out of the water. Of course, we have to start somewhere – so **start** with what you **think** will be the most successful and branch out from there, but test everything.

MORE KPI

Instagram ads are cheaper than Facebook ads. Facebook ads are significantly cheaper than LinkedIn ads. A low budget LinkedIn ad campaign will be cheaper than a radio ad ...and so on.

You might get 3 sales per week on Instagram that cost you £60 each to acquire, you might only get 1 per week on LinkedIn that cost you £100.

"Not only are my ads cheaper on Instagram – I'm getting more sales! Instagram is better for my business model."

What if, due to the differing demographics your average sale on Instagram is £2,000, but LinkedIn's average is £10,000. LinkedIn might cost more and get you fewer sales, but what's better now, when you actually measure the data?

£60 for a £2,000 sale

or

£100 for a £10,000 sale?

PUSH OR PULL?

Another thing to think about is that ads can be broken in to two categories – **Push** or **Pull**.

Push ads are when you're pushing your product on a potential customer. So, the Teespring t-shirts in the story previously would be a good example of that. Likewise, a Personal Trainer looking for new clients, a jeweller selling their creations at any time or perhaps running a promotion around a particular holiday like Christmas or Valentine's Day.

…but what if you have a removal company? What if you are an emergency plumber? Are people scrolling their Facebook feed while their kitchen floods in the background? How can you push a product that people only need when they **need** it?

That is where you have **Pull**. Pull is when someone is actively looking for a service and you appear. When someone searches for a removal service on Google **that is likely the very moment they are ready to buy**. They've already put themselves out there and you just have to **Pull** them in. You can **Push** advertising for an Emergency Plumber, but you then have to hope they keep your information somehow in the event of an emergency. 99% of the time you would be **Pulling** them in when they're currently in the middle of an emergency.

Pull is easier to convert because the potential customer is already proactively looking for the product or service. They are already a warm lead – you just have to reel them into you over any of your competition.

However, most of the time you have to Push because chances are, they don't know they need the product or service until you show them!

Most businesses can be both though, and it's important to have a healthy combination of Push and Pull for businesses that can service both as part of your marketing suite.

You should be exploring both Push and Pull and finding out what works best. Keep an eye on your Cost Per Acquisition (CPA) and find the medium for you.

The only exception to this is if you know that your CLV (Customer Lifetime Value) is worth far more than just the initial sale. Spending £100 to acquire a £50 sale is still fine if 90% of your customers take your £500 upsell afterwards, or simply buy again, or go on to make regular monthly payments, or if 90% of them refer 2 friends …and so on.

WHAT ARE THEY SEARCHING FOR?

Much like finding out where your clients are, you also need to find out what they're searching for. You need find out the language and terminology they use, because it might not be the same as you.

A client (who has now become a very good friend) originally contacted me many years ago to improve his Search Engine Ranking for potential clients searching for *"Computer Support"* in our city. Once we crunched the numbers, we discovered that literally 10 times the amount of Googles users had been searching for *"IT Support"*. We covered both, but you can likely tell which one we focussed on!

You must understand where your clients are looking and the exact language they're using. This is essential in Copywriting, but we'll get to that later.

OPT INS

What is an **Opt In**? When you exchange your email address for information on a website - this is an Opt In. It might just be a subscription to a newsletter, or it might be for something like an eBook that has useful information. The trade-off is that you are given something of value in exchange for allowing the company to contact you with some sort of frequency.

Now, almost every business should be collecting customer emails and encouraging them to agree to be contacted. As I'll go into more detail later - your email list is a fantastic tool for getting customers to spend more when they do actually buy, encouraging them to buy more frequently and also encouraging their friends to buy, too.

Opt ins can be important depending on the industry you are in, but what's more important than me telling you how to do it is, again, understanding the principals so you can apply those principals to more than just opt ins.

Give your potential customers what they want – not what you want to give them.

Those that get the best results from Opt Ins, I'm talking the results the 1%'ers get - come from businesses that deliver massive value:

- Up front.
- For free.

The other 99% are given some tokenistic garbage, masquerading as value that's designed to scam you out of your email address. This will lose all good will and turn you right off their sales pitch. Remember this is often the first thing a potential customer will receive from you - make sure it's of quality.

You could give 90% of your knowledge away and sell the remaining 10% once you've delivered value, proven your expertise and shown your potential client or customer that working with you is irresistible. You know your stuff, your product's excellent, you've walked the walk, there's no risk for you or the client.

This scares business owners. They think guarding the secrets of their product or service is how you make the customer feel like they **need** you. Have you heard of the internet? People will find out whatever they want. They are however – lazy.

People will choose convenience over everything.

Don't fear giving anything away. The ones that run away and try to do it themselves are usually cheap and not worth fighting for. Rely on potential customers that, when you give your value then say:

"I trust you now – do it all for me anyway."

A good example would be Dog Walkers selling walks, daycare, drop-ins and so on.

I've learned that for good dog walking companies there's more to walking a dog than turning up with a lead and strolling down the path. It's hugely advantageous to understand *'Dog Psychology'*. If you understand why a dog behaves the way it does you can tailor your own behaviour and your walks accordingly, meaning both you and the dogs will have a better experience. Happier dogs, happier owners, happier you.

Does *"Choosing A Good Dog Walker"* sound like a good idea for an Opt In …from a company that's trying to sell you a dog walking service? The old 80's style sales leaflet of *"8 Things You Should Look For When Buying…"* where you, funnily enough, go through a list of things that go in your businesses favour - isn't going to cut it here.

How about:

"Doggy Psychology – Understand Your Dog & Strengthen Your Bond"

Does that sound like something a dog owner might be interested in? Is it something that delivers real value?

…but wait! If I teach them the psychology and make walks better and more fun for them, they won't need me!

"Haha, now you've given away all your secrets you fool! Off I go to apply them all by myself where you will receive zero money!"

Runs away wearing a mask and holding a giant SWAG bag

If this is your thinking, you should revaluate your business model. Your job as a business is to deliver value and be a worthwhile investment. Help people, deliver value and the money will always follow. The above eBook would do far more for your reputation and your potential customers belief in your ability to deliver.

What if your industry isn't as fun or consumable as dog walking? Something more matter-of-fact and process driven? Let's say a Gas Engineer – boiler installation, repairs, maintenance, servicing and so on. Not only this, but as we discussed earlier that this business can often lean more towards Pull marketing, rather than Push. It's hard to sell a boiler until someone reaches the point they really need a new one. What kind of opt in could you do for this?

We've already covered *"How To Choose The Right Boiler Installer"* isn't going to cut it. What delivers real, honest, genuine value?

What about: *"How To Service Your Own Boiler"*? A little risky given there's electricity and gas involved, and it would likely only appeal to a small group of people who were willing to do DIY on a boiler. You're getting the idea and thinking along the right lines though.

How about:

"6 Easy Hacks To Cut Down Your Boilers Energy Consumption"

Now we're talking. Delivers value, saves money every month and is easily consumable. But we're still in the Pull space, so how does this help business?

Who do the people that downloaded this handy eBook think of when they need anything to do with their boiler? You could even leave a well-designed pamphlet as a nice touch with every new boiler install for the customer to pass on to their family and friends.

That's just for eBooks too! Opt ins could be:

- A video or video series.
- Some sort of membership access.
- A trial of your software.

There are so many different opportunities to deliver value and showcase your expertise. Think carefully about your opt in. I've never came across an industry I wasn't able to come up with something that delivers genuine customer value.

WAIT, YOU'RE NOT BUILDING A LIST YET?

The best time to be building a list was yesterday!

The number one thing successful online business owners say is their biggest regret?

"Not building a list sooner."

You likely fit into 1 of 3 camps:

1. What is a list?
2. I've been meaning to do it. I want to do it. I understand the importance of it. I tried it once.
3. I've been growing my list, marketing to my list, learning, making loads of sales and winning at life.

If you don't know what building a list is: It's increasing the amount or quality of emails you have from people who are likely to be good customers of yours …and there's many effective ways to do it.

When someone subscribes to your list you know they're interested in your particular product.

Think about it - if you advertise on TV, radio, print or other traditional mediums you're only hitting a fraction of the demographic that's actually interested in what you do. If someone opts in to your email list, you **know** they like or need your product or service.

It's almost 100% targeted marketing.

Once you have a customer or potential customers email (providing you're giving good value) you can remarket to them again and again. Most of the biggest digital start-ups in the last 10 years generate over **90% of their revenue** through emails.

Email is one of the most personal marketing mediums: You're in a client's hand, speaking to them directly through their inbox. Also, through forwarding or sharing - clients can also promote what you've sent them, giving you an even bigger reach.

Email has high open rate too, all for a very cheap *'cost per person'* interaction. A Facebook post currently has a reach of about **2%** to your *'Likers'*, and you'll need to pay to *'Boost'* a post to get that percentage any further.

Email has over 70%

Another essential benefit ...and I can't stress this enough, is you also **own** your list! This may sound strange but in other mediums like social media, you're at the mercy of how these companies operate. They change the rules all the time. As I mentioned before; companies go down the tube solely based on Facebook changing their adverts terms of service, meaning the company can't bring in new business like it used to. Same for Search Engine Optimisation – a simple Google algorithm change can ruin a whole business model.

Own your list.

No one can take it away from you. Users can unsubscribe, but that's squarely on you and the quality of your content.

Also, people don't always check their social media, but they almost always get around to checking their email. It doesn't get lost in the fog either - it'll be there whenever they decide to pick it up, which is the reason behind the **70%** figure above.

Your list size isn't necessarily important either. I've seen lists of under 100 steamroll lists of thousands in terms of engagement and sales. What's a client worth to you? I have a client where a new client to them can be worth over £10,000 every year. A very tight and targeted list of a few hundred is gold dust to them.

As I mentioned earlier, you can set your potential clients up on a sequence of emails after an opt in to tell a story, to prove your worth in reference to the problems your business or product solves.

You can give your subscribers special offers or *'first access'* to a new product or service you're launching. If you create a new product or service from scratch or launch a new arm to your existing business providing it's industry relevant - what's better:

Building customers from scratch?

or

Having an existing bank of emails you can market to from day one?

You can test different types of emails, different styles, different language, different calls to action and places to click to. Given all the metrics available you can find out what works best based on each receivers' behaviour. You can then do more of what works best to get better results each time. Get feedback from your receivers and you'll learn more about your potential clients and how better to approach them on other mediums – even in real life!

Where should you be asking for emails?

- On your website.
- On your blog posts.
- In your social media.
- In your social media advertising.
- By hand on any forms you give out, at say, your events.
- Ask those who give you their business card if they would like to be added.

The list is almost endless.

Also be sure if it's relevant to you, that you're complying with GDPR (General Data Protection Regulation) or any other laws of the countries you'll be collecting emails from. Make sure you can prove you received their email as an opt in and didn't blindly add them to your list without permission. You also need to show where subscribers data is stored if you are audited and that it can be removed or deleted easily if the subscriber requests it.

This book was released post-GDPR, otherwise your email list could've potentially fallen into the same principal as relying on one medium and having it taken away from you.

Businesses that were perhaps very small and built their email lists up through face to face interactions; receiving business cards; interacting with clients and getting verbal approvals to send emails – now with tighter GDPR laws they have no proof those people on that list consented to being sent emails.

So, these businesses have email lists of hundreds, perhaps thousands of previous clients, existing clients and connections they've made that they market to regularly - it could be a huge part of their business. Now because they don't have a digital paper trail for the consent, they need to send a GDPR approval email where their contacts must click through and accept. The problem with this is apathy. These consent emails are not those on the email lists' number one priority, so those that don't even mind receiving the emails read it while doing other things and forget to click through.

Now that small business owner has a list 10% of the size it once was!

That list is probably tighter now in terms of targeting and those that are undoubtedly interested, but what about those that only felt a little interested, didn't mind receiving the emails but never got round to the approving the consent and were regular or at least occasional buyers? The difference in the lifetime value of that list could be that business owners' entire mortgage!

What if you are a much bigger company with a much bigger list and the way you used to collect emails didn't have historical data about the consent, or the consent wasn't worded in a way that GDPR requires? A hammer-blow to your business.

Even email isn't immune to relying on one source for all of your business, so make sure your GDPR consent is tight, even if it doesn't apply to your country – because rest assured it could one day in the not too distant future.

To sum up, email is:

- Personal.
- Direct.
- Private.
- The most effective in terms of reach.
- 100% targeted.
- Used to market to your list again and again with current or new services and products.
- Used to get more sales.
- Used to get new customers.
- Used to increase traffic.
- ...and most important of all, you **own** your list!

So, it's one of the most effective, if not the most. It's one of the cheapest. It's one of the most personal and the most targeted because the person has voluntarily joined your list thus displaying their interest in your product or service. It has an infinite lifespan, providing your subscribers don't unsubscribe and it can be started with a tiny existing list.

So, why are you not building a list?

FUNNELS

What is a funnel? Well, it's basically the sales process you take someone through, from potential customer to paying customer. As I've mentioned before – selling to a cold audience is tough, so you have to warm them up somehow. You have to build trust and give value.

Your funnel could be as simple as:

Website > Opt in > Sales Email

It could also be:

Advert > Website > Retargeting Advert > Sales Page > Opt In > 12 automated, value delivering emails across a specific timeframe > Sales Email

Why stop there? The funnel can then branch out into:

- What happens when that specific person doesn't buy? Offer them a down-sell!
- What happens if they do buy? Offer them an up-sell.
- What happens if they buy that, too?!

Funnels can be as simple or as complicated as you like. You can start small and build it out from there. If you're completely new to it, you can create a free or paid account from a bulk email service provider such as MailChimp. Then, keep it simple by using their own opt in forms that when someone puts in their email address, they get an automatic email with the opt in. Add that to your website and you can start collecting emails from potential clients.

Once you're gathering the data of what works you can branch out into more sophisticated systems. You can build everything yourself or you can buy the more complex software for example ClickFunnels and Leadpages which both have click and drag funnel builders that take all of the heavy lifting out of it.

Just like all the advice in this book – act on it yourself, take the time, research, study, act, improve or pay someone to do it for you. There are freelancers who do nothing but build funnels, full time. Hire them on one of the freelancing websites like Upwork or PeoplePerHour. If your business or idea isn't particularly complicated there will be off the shelf solutions that these freelancers can plug you into without you paying for a bespoke solution.

RETARGETING & THE '*TOUCH PRINCIPAL*'

Retargeting has become arguably the most important strategy for marketing on the web in recent years. As I'll keep repeating, people rarely buy right away - unless you're Coca-Cola.

Know why people buy Coca-Cola? Because it tastes good? Because it gives you energy and alertness? Maybe.

The main reason:

No matter what where you buy it, anywhere in the world – it's the same.

A Coke bought in the UK is the same as in the US and is the same in South East Asia. You could discover a wooden shack on a dirt road in a Brazilian jungle that sells Coke from their fridge and it will taste exactly as you've always known it to. People like to know what they're getting when they buy something.

When someone tries the latest marketing avenue, like the Facebook Ads example I mentioned previously - then they say it doesn't work; they don't understand human behaviour.

Promoting your product or service to a cold audience that have never seen you or your brand before is a tough gig. People have more choice than ever nowadays, they have the ability to research you first, they have a stronger bullshit'ometer than ever before.

The right sales copy to the right people can always overcome it, but since you're probably not a master copywriter - to make things easier you need to work on your **touch principal**.

Depending on who you listen to (and this'll vary from type of product to customer demographic) there's between 6 to 12 touches a consumer needs to have before they buy your product.

What is a **touch**? This is what it would have looked like back in the day:

- Someone might see your ad on TV.
- Get in their car and drive past your billboard.
- Listen to your radio ad.
- Open their newspaper and see an ad or article about your product.
- Go to the water cooler, where their colleague starts a conversation about your product.
- On the way home they see the billboard again.
- Listen to the radio ad again...

...and so on. Each one of those is a *'touch'*.

So, what is the modern-day Touch Principal for a small business owner?

Retargeting.

Retargeting is a pixel (a small piece of code) set up on your website that gathers data about a visitor. Google has it for their Ads and most of the major social platforms have their own individual ones.

If it's a Google pixel for example; Google can gather the data of the person that visited your website and serve them adverts as they surf around the web. Ever noticed when you go on most websites these days that the ads are tailored to a product you've just been looking at? That's Retargeting.

The website you're visiting effectively has blank ad space and the data gathered from pixels around the web populates those ad spaces. It's the same with the Facebook tracking pixel. Looking at vacuum cleaners on Amazon and jackets on ASOS? All of a sudden you get ads for both when scrolling through your Facebook news feed.

Someone has proven they are interested in your product by the virtue of visiting your website, and given that they are unlikely to buy first time because of the Touch Principal - you can have 100% targeted marketing to semi-qualified leads (only serving ads to those that have a proven interest in your product or service) and infinitely more touches, just by retargeting.

What's more:

You're only charged when someone takes action on your ad.

Meaning you're not paying for the space like traditional advertising – you're only paying when someone clicks on the ad. No wastage and only paying for any interest generated. So, for those that don't click – it's a free *'touch'*.

Start using pixels as soon as possible. You can install them and gather the data without paying for ads. They don't just pull the Google, Facebook, LinkedIn etc. account of the user, but the demographics and what those people *'Like'* and build a profile of the type of people that are most interested in your product. Then when you **do** decide to start running the ads – you've got a ready-made list of warm prospects (given they've visited your website at some point already, or they match the behaviours of those that have visited your website).

Not only this, but based on the demographics of that list you can build a *'Lookalike Audience'* and target those that have the same interests as your list, allowing you to reach out further based on behaviour, rather than a completely cold audience.

"My clients aren't on Facebook!"

First of all, save your assumptions. Test! Even if you don't think your clients are on Facebook, set up a pixel only to do retargeting ads because the ones that have visited your website clearly are.

You can start using a pixel right away. Even if your website is new you could run an ad to a cold audience, then providing the pixel is set up on your website it'll gather the data of those that are interested on some level. Retarget to those visitors – you now have a ready-made list of warm leads almost off the bat!

MOMENTUM

You must keep your marketing efforts going. Any time you stop, you lose all your momentum and it's like starting from scratch every time.

Your ad quality score will suffer on Pay Per Click, your algorithmic improvements will suffer in SEO and your Facebook Ad optimisation (done by Facebook themselves) will be lost. All the money and time you invested could potentially be wasted.

It's imperative that you maintain your online ad presence, as getting results right away is rarely the case. You must build a brand, authority and be regularly seen.

Gather momentum, month on month, otherwise you'll be starting from scratch again, spending another £40 on ads and telling me in polite conversation that you've tried it already but it *"doesn't work"*.

CASE STUDIES

Case studies always trump explaining what you do. If you can produce detailed case studies and get them in front of a similar audience to that case study – you will get customers.

As long as your product or service is good you will get customers:

"Here's what I did for a business, or someone the same as you, therefore I can get you similar results."

If you have impressive clients - it's extremely important to leverage them to get more of the same businesses in those industries.

The less you niche-down on your case studies the more catch-all they'll be, but if you niche-down you'll get more of your ideal customers – and they'll pay more.

Build multiple, detailed case studies for:

- Specific industries you focus on.
- Customer demographics.
- Individual services you provide.

Like:

- Facebook ads, for burger joints, in Brooklyn.
- Getting back into shape, for women in their 30's, who've just had a kid.
- Bar services, for non-alcoholic cocktails, served at Muslim weddings.

A single company doing one for each of its services and demographics could look like this:

- Pensions for 30-something's who haven't thought about doing it yet.

- Pensions for 40-year-old men looking to switch and get more from their provider.
- Pensions for 50-year-old divorced women who want the highest monthly yield.
- Investments for 25-year-old, app start-up founders in Silicon Valley that have just sold their company.
- Investments for 40-year-olds that inherit large sums.
- Investments for 50 to 60-year-old hard savers.
- Life Insurance for women starting new families.
- Wills and Power of Attorney for those with terminal illness.

Each of these as an individual case study with the real-life customer. You want your potential customers to put themselves in the case studies shoes. The more they can do this – the more likely they will be to contact you.

As a few examples, I have a personal training client called Paul. Paul likes doing free workshops for companies in Scotland with professionals that don't have a lot of spare time but want to eat better, feel better, move better and fit exercise into their busy schedule. He enjoys it as it's part of his **why** in giving health advice and helping as many people as he can lead a healthier life. Often as a result of this, those in his audience become clients.

So, how did we market that?

1. Build an excellent case study around one of the most successful workshops he had with a major city law firm.
2. On LinkedIn; invite to connect with those in his target demographic (in this instance: Scottish law firm owners / Partners / HR).
3. Those that connect back are sent a personalised message with a link to the case study on his website.

When Paul started working with me, he had himself and one other trainer doing 30 sessions per month. He was getting 1 or 2 sign ups per month offline and around **5 per year** online.

After working with me he now has himself and 3 trainers doing 70 to 80 sessions per month, and he's looking to take on another trainer.

It's not uncommon for Paul to convert 4 new clients per week, with one week's leads recently converting to £1,000 per month in business.

I did the same thing for my dentist client, Mark who branched out into a mobile care home service where we wrote a detailed case study on how his service helped care home owners.

After only a few months he had to employ and train more staff to cope with the demand!

The right message, at the right time, to the right people.

Case studies should focus on:

1. **The Challenge** – A background of the customer, what they're looking to improve. In Paul's case it was to improve the health of their staff, reduce sick days, lower stress, increase focus, productivity and performance, greater staff satisfaction and create a positive corporate image.

2. **The Solution** – A detailed account of what you did. In Mark's case he provided a service that visited care homes, his company did all the paperwork, kept the customer compliant around care home oral hygiene and oral cancer checks, drastically improving the care homes audit scores and also organised all return visits to carry out simple treatments. Meaning care home managers no longer had to worry about anything – it was all taken out of their hands.

3. **The Results** – Words on what the solution achieved, including direct quotes from the customers.

All of this designed as a page on your website with a strong call to action. It can also be repurposed on social media, email, presentations, shown in meetings and used in direct messaging as shown in the instances above.

REFERRALS

The only thing more powerful than a case study or a testimonial? A person that someone else trusts recommending your business to them.

The amazing thing about this is that although this book is full of things you could and should be doing to grow your business – you have no control over this most effective form of marketing.

...or do you?

People will naturally talk about you if you're doing a good job for them - but you shouldn't rely on this happening by chance. First of all, as I mention throughout the book, having a good business and doing a good job is the most important thing – it makes everything else, including this, much easier.

It is extremely unlikely that your product or service **never** comes up in conversation. When it does, you want to make sure that your customer or client is singing your praises, then if the person they are talking to needs that product or service – chances are they'll use you. You'll trip over these referrals from time to time, but you should want to actively encourage those conversations.

Most clients won't refer you. Not because you didn't do a good job - it's that it often never enters their minds.

Like I mentioned in asking for case studies and testimonials – are you asking for referrals? You've done a good job, there's no harm at all in asking for referrals – it's good business practice. You could literally just ask them face to face or on the phone:

"Do you know anyone <product> could help?"
"Do you know anyone else that could use my services?"
"Do you have any friends, family or colleagues that could use the same thing?"

…and so on.

You could send an email to each and every customer after you've fulfilled an order, or after a period of time working with you that you feel has been a beneficial period for them.

You can also incentivise them in some way, so they get a discount on their own orders. But really, as humans, just the endorphins of helping you (who has done a good job for them) and the person they refer is enough – studies have shown that incentives are rarely necessary, particularly when it's B2B.

These are just some examples. The truth is it'll vary heavily from business to business how you think it's best to bring the suggestion up in terms of place, time and platform.

Whatever it is - make it part of your routine. Again, it's not that your customers don't want to refer – it's that you're not their priority and they've not really thought about it. 9 times out of 10 you simply have to ask, then they'll be more than happy to help you or your company.

WHO'S SELLING?

There's no use having good leads if you or your team is shit at selling.

How to sell is littered throughout this book, but I'm talking specifically about whose job it is to convert leads, regardless if those leads come from:

- Face to face meetings.
- Telephone enquiries.
- Contact form submissions.
- Email enquiries.
- Social media messages.

Is the right person handling those? Do they have training? Do they have a loose script to follow? A known pattern of language that handles and converts typical objections? Are they friendly, engaging and knowledgeable about your product?

Are you spending money on advertising, generating leads, then rubbishing those leads as *'low quality'* – or do you have low quality converters at your end? I've trained countless members of staff that unwittingly put off potential leads that are virtually begging to be sold to.

If this is happening, then you are wasting advertising money!

Low quality leads are undoubtedly a thing. I'm not talking about dragging a timewaster who has no interest in buying through a sales process – but, as I mentioned before; if you're asking a staff member or outsourcer to care as much about your business as you do (when it doesn't affect what they get paid at the end of the month)...

You better get them trained, because they won't make the effort off their own back unless they're given structure on what to say and how to say it.

Does the person who handles phone enquiries have the same training as the person answering Facebook messages? Because what you do, and the way you say it, is handled differently on different platforms. In fact, you could be dealing with completely different demographics depending on what platform each choose to consume your information on and then contact you on that platform.

Ensure whoever is handling your leads is either properly trained or it is outsourced to a professional.

PREDICTIONS

It's always risky taking predictions out of your head and into print, particularly in the only book you might end up writing! I have claims and predictions across many of the sections in this book, but here's a couple that don't fit in anywhere.

One of the biggest predictions I see happening - is the big social platforms offering its users a subscription service for their own content. This isn't really a prediction in the sense that some platforms have already begun testing it – but from a business point of view it could be one of the biggest and most lucrative changes for content creators.

Right now, the biggest service for voluntary donations is Patreon.

With Patreon you can crowd-fund your content. Meaning the general public or your *'fans'* pay to see your content – the understanding being they really like whatever it is you produce (video, art, writing, music, podcasts) but you can't work for free if you were to do it full time.

There are different levels (or *'Tiers'*) set by each creator which can get you various things like:

- Early access to content.
- Donation only content.
- Shout-outs on podcasts or videos.
- Discounts on products.
- A personal illustration commissioned of you.

...and so on. Almost anything you want to give, in exchange for a monthly payment.

I absolutely love this, as you can be paid (with all the fulfilment handled by Patreon for a small cut) for doing what you love, effortlessly over the internet. If your content is good – people can vote for it with their cash, without the need of middle men (well, Patreon take their cut, but I mean in terms of publishers or studios).

Anyway, that's a lot of context for what is a simple prediction:

The likes of Facebook and YouTube are already testing the donation / tier model and I think this will completely revolutionise everything in content creation. I think there will be a much bigger swell, even more than the obvious *"oh, I might as well utilise that as part of the platform offering it"* for subscription-based content creation. I think there will be a whole new industry starting it or moving to it en masse.

The ratio of content creators to content creators monetising on Patreon will currently be quite a big gap, because someone has to leave the place the content is being viewed (Facebook, YouTube etc.) go on to Patreon, sign up, put in their payment details and so on.

There are too many steps and a lot of creators will lose out due to that apathy. Yes, you can view the content on Patreon – but it's the kind of extra steps creators won't set up and most of the public won't jump through those hoops to get to it. Plus, Patreon doesn't have a fraction of the user base Facebook and YouTube has.

YouTube offering a subscription model for its creators' fans and Facebook offering subscriptions for, say, private group owners to put a paywall around their community.

…and the user doesn't need to leave the platform to subscribe. They might even have their payment details stored already from previous transactions.

I think this will be huge. Bigger than it's even being imagined.

My other prediction is the growth of Virtual Reality (VR). It's been threatening to go mainstream for as long as I can remember, but nobody had really cracked it. We're seeing a fair bit of traction now, with VR headsets and software / games now being affordable. You don't even need fancy hardware or an expensive, powerful PC to run it – they have VR headset for your PlayStation that can cost less than the system itself and headsets for your phone that cost even less than that.

The sensory experience even for the average consumer is incredible.

The more mainstream it gets, the more it will replace real interaction. It's mostly seen as an entertainment device for gaming at the moment, but it will easily move into the likes of education, boardrooms and more extreme escapism for the likes of relationships or hugely extended periods like holidays. In the future, why buy an expensive houses or holidays if you can imitate the experience through VR?

We're getting worse with our attachment to phones. As someone who enjoys human interaction and finds those constantly on their phone total dicks, I worry about how this won't just be used to help those with anxiety and other genuine mental and physical health issues. In fact, it will likely lead us to further isolation the better it gets – especially if we can create environments around us that are better than some people's reality.

In spite of my soapbox, the main reason for mentioning it is - could you be an early adopter? With every iteration of new internet technology and its accompanying software - there has been a gold rush, where the early adopters have gotten a head start, or made a name for themselves, or bought ads when they were cheap.

With social platforms offering subscription models for content creators - how can you monetise your service on there?

How can you innovate and make sure yours is the VR product they use?

OK, now we're going to get a little more specific around current platforms and methods, but it's important to note – I can only go into so much detail here. I'll give an overview of each method, how it helps and advice for best practices. The nuts and bolts of what buttons to press can be found all over YouTube and going into the specifics of each one could fill a book on their own. If you don't understand something - ask.

SEO

(Search Engine Optimisation)

When anyone searches for something on Google, the results are organised by how Google thinks they should rank based on how helpful those websites are to the search query.

I say Google rather than *"search engines"* a lot because it has literally 90% of the market share. There is a market for ranking on other search engines, particularly targeting older people who tend to use whatever generic browser is on their computer system – but if we were gonna go that deep, this section could be a book in its own right.

In an ideal world (for Google) this would be a completely natural process, where their bots (known as spiders) crawl all the sites on the web. Based on Google's ever-changing algorithm - the system decides what each of those websites should rank highest for.

The goal is to get the number 1 slot on Google for your preferred term, or at the very least on page 1. Each page has 10 results on it, so anything like: *"Lawyer in New York"* is extremely competitive, whereas *"Lawyer in <insert remote town of 1,000 people>"* is not competitive. Of course, less competition often means lower volume of searches being made for that term.

Taking it further – Google samples the data of its users' behaviour. To keep it simple: If people are searching Google for a particular term and you are 8th on the first page, and one of your competitors is 7th, but the searchers are clicking more often on **your** website instead of your competitors and are staying to find the information they need, not clicking back on the browser – Google takes that data and decides you should be at least above your competitor. This is all happening as a stream of data for Google, and rankings change constantly, automatically.

Statistics show, unless you're a household name like Coca-Cola, a potential customer is 80% likely to Google you before making a buying decision. Meaning it's important to at least have your website ranked for your own business name.

What I typically do for a client that hasn't yet established themselves in the search engines is:

- Begin ranking their company name.
- Then their service and local area.
- Then move in a circular radius outward from there.

Again, keeping it very simple:

"Lawyer <insert very small town or area of a town>"
"Lawyer <larger town>"
"Lawyer <city or region>"
"Lawyer <country>"

"Lawyer <anything>" is going to be tough, particularly if you're starting with a new website and no ranking history, so it's important to do your Keyword Research to find out what Google users in the area you're targeting are searching for.

I'm not going to get into the nuts and bolts of how you do it (as I mentioned: How to do something that is only process driven can be found during a quick Google/YouTube search) but there are tools out there that will give you the data on what has been searched on Google in any area of the world – this is called Keyword Research.

I remind you of the instance I mentioned before, when my client originally wanted to rank highly on Google for *"Computer Support"* when the term *"IT Support"* had over 10 times the number of searches based on the data.

Do your keyword research and find out what your potential customers are searching for on Google. Build pages on your website dedicated to those keywords and services, much like the demographics mentioned in the Case Studies section previously – but this time with the Keyword Research data.

Remember, *"Lawyer <anything>"* is competitive and vague. There might be a lot of people searching for it but most of your traffic will come from more obscure and less obvious terms. That coupled with data that shows someone searching for: *"Nike Trainers"* is a lot less primed to make a buying decision than someone searching: *"Nike Air Max Black Size 10"*.

Be more specific in your targeting, because there might be a really competitive keyword that has 100,000 searches per month but it's extremely difficult to rank for and has a bunch of *'window shoppers'* searching for it. Whereas another, more specific or niche keyword in the same industry and area has only 20 searches per month… but you can rank number 1 on Google for it with much less competition …and 5 of those monthly searchers end up buying from you.

Depending on the industry, 5 sales per month might be huge... and that's just for 1 keyword. You could literally rank for thousands of keywords.

If you are a tradesman that does one job per day: Without factoring in repeat business or referrals - you only need 20 customers per month.

That's just SEO for location related terms. If you have a business where you can ship to anywhere, or a consultancy that can work, say, anywhere in the English-speaking world; then the search net is even wider, no longer constrained to specific geographical locations.

So, how do you do it? Again, a lot of it is process driven but SEO can be broken down into two parts: On Site SEO and Off Site SEO.

On Site is doing everything you can to show the search engines that your website is relevant to a particular search term or keyword. This means typing your headings, descriptions, page titles, meta descriptions, naming your images, making sure the text in your website says the keywords you want to rank for often, and so on. You tailor everything on your website to the keywords that you're targeting.

Don't worry if that sounds complicated, there's plenty of tools and plugins out there to literally type in the relevant boxes what you want if you're not willing to pay for a professional or can't afford to just yet. The plugins will give you an overall rating as to how well you've done in your On Site SEO and suggests specific changes to make in order to improve it.

On Site SEO is also about creating good content. Blog posts, images, videos, sales pages and so on that are genuinely helpful to the end user (your potential customer). Remember, Google has a very sophisticated algorithm that's getting better all the time. If you're creating content your potential customers will like Google will see that and rank you higher accordingly because:

They are looking to create the best, most efficient experience for their user.

This is often why websites have Blogs or News sections, as it allows the owners to be constantly creating fresh content, targeting new and existing keywords – further illustrating to Google that the website is a great source of information for specific search terms.

Off Site SEO is arguably more important, given the power of backlinks. A backlink is a link to your website on another website. The authority and industry relevance of that website determines the power of that backlink, which in turn determines your ranking for a keyword.

For example, back in the day the **number** of backlinks was the most important:

More backlinks = more people effectively *'vouching'* for your website.

However, that just meant companies would set up a bunch of websites, typically overseas that were used for nothing other than linking to websites that people paid to have their links on.

Fast forward to today and this is easily spotted by Google. Now, the most important factors are the ranking, authority and relevance of the backlinking website.

Extreme examples from each end of the spectrum would be: If you are Jill, a Financial Adviser in the UK and you have 2 backlinks linking to your website:

- **Backlink 1** is your aunt Maisie who lives in the US and has a bakery hobby website and wants to support her niece, putting Jill's web address somewhere on her website.

- **Backlink 2** is an interview Jill did for the Finance section of the BBC website, where at the end of the article they say *"If you would like to learn more about Jill, you can contact her here"* (where *"here"* is a link to Jill's website).

Backlink 1 is from a small website, who's server is across the Atlantic from Jill's, that has no authority, and potentially no links to it. It also has nothing to do with finance in any way.

Backlink 2 is from one of the biggest websites in the world, a trusted source with millions of articles, millions of backlinks linking to it and a high PR (Page Rank). It's an article page all about a finance topic and it's in the Finance section of the BBC - so is incredibly relevant to Jill's websites' industry and the location of the BBC's website server is likely in the same country as Jill's.

Backlink 2 will be giving Jill incredible *'link juice'*, but backlink 1 is still important because Jill's *'backlink profile'* should look natural, diverse and *'real'*.

Social Backlinks are becoming more important all of the time. Just as they sound, these are links to your website that are on the social media channels. Social media can also be *'gamed'* but when it's not gamed there's no truer barometer for Google as to how genuinely useful or engaging your content is to the public.

Your anchor text is also very important. I don't want to get too technical as the How-To can be found all over YouTube, but it's worth mentioning that anchor text plays a big part. Anchor text is what the actual link to your website says. So, in the example of Backlink 2:

"If you would like to learn more about Jill, you can contact her here".

162

"Here" is the Anchor Text because that's the link (typically in blue and underlined). If that whole sentence was a blue, underlined hyperlink then that itself would be the Anchor Text.

Anchor Text is better if it's the actual keyword you're targeting. So, rather than *"here"*, or *"click here"*, or *"www.jillfinancialadviser.com"*, it would ideally be *"Financial Advice London"* if that's what you're trying to rank for.

Again though, diversity is important. If all of your backlinks are *"Financial Advice London"* then it'll look contrived and unnatural to Google when their system audits your website. Make sure there's plenty of variety in there, but the most common ones should be the keywords you're looking to rank for and pointing to the relevant pages on your website.

There are free and paid tools to see what the Backlink Profile is of your website. The Backlink Profile is the number of links to your website and then a broken down summary of what each one is. From there you can start fixing existing ones. You might know or be able to contact the website owner / editor of the pages / articles that have your backlink on them. If you feel they're being harmful – have them removed. If they look good - then you can ask to have the anchor text changed to something you prefer.

Not only can you produce content for your own website, you can guest post on other websites. From companies in the same or similar niche to you that you've built up a relationship with, to relevant news sites who are always looking for articles. You can write an article and email it out to the editor of multiple websites – asking who wants to run it.

The most important thing in SEO though, for a long, sustainable business model is:

Good quality content.

Think about it, even if all you do for years is create content (providing it's genuinely really useful insightful, engaging content) the backlinks will come naturally through visitors wanting to share that great content. Website editors could even come to you and ask you to write something for them in exchange for exposure and a backlink.

SEO should be the additional work that gets already great content noticed and under the noses of the right people.

Although Google has caught up with random websites backlinking to your website - you can still buy backlinks from private networks. *'Secret'* networks of websites that are all on unique servers, attempting to look natural. Those websites themselves have many other websites linking to them and have built up high Page Ranks as a result - so you can pay to have your website address placed on them with a relevantly written article and Anchor Text of your choice, thus gaming the system.

This is called *"Black Hat"* SEO, whereas doing your own On Site SEO correctly and creating honest content is considered *"White Hat"* SEO.

If you're deliberately asking companies for specific Anchor Texts and actively pursuing links from other websites, then it's not *'natural'* and technically *"Grey Hat"* (a term that's actually used).

The truth is – it depends what you're trying to do. If you wanted to ride the crest of the wave when Fidget Spinners became hugely popular in 2017 and needed your Fidget Spinner eCommerce website to rank quickly and you have a genuine *'In and Out'* strategy, then it's no big deal. If you're doing it with your brand, which you plan to grow and build a solid reputation that you'll keep forever - then it's a bad idea. If Google decides your links are bullshit, they'll remove your website from the rankings, tanking your organic traffic in one move.

This can sometimes be recovered with a combination of the backlink profile tools I mentioned earlier and the Google Disavow tool - but really, I don't want to get into that because you hopefully never find yourself in that situation.

Most business owners don't have the discipline to create consistently good content, but it's always the answer – and it's always been the answer. It isn't just better rankings – one of the by-products is when anyone visits your website for any reason, they instantly improve their opinion of you. You must carve yourself out as an authority in your industry (and preferably your specific niche) – this is where customers will pick you over a competitor.

It's extremely hard to discipline yourself to do it, but 1 or 2 hours a week dedicated to content creation will be incredible over a year when you have 50 new articles, written by you on your website that you can then repurpose across social, email, make a course, write a book and so on - in order to maximise your exposure and authority. The task is not difficult, it's the discipline that's hard – but it's what will separate you from your competition.

Also, if your business address is publicly displayed it's important to claim your business on the Google My Business (GMB) platform. When you do a search for most things that do (or can) have premises like lawyers, garages, restaurants etc. often at the top (or near the top) of a Google search is what's currently known as (at time of writing, because these sorts of things can change) the 3-Pack. The 3-Pack is the top 3 listings on the Google Places listings, which is a map with markers down, indicating where the businesses addresses are.

It's free, and a well filled out GMB profile will go a long way to improve your ranking and increase your exposure to searchers – particularly if you make it into that elusive 3-Pack.

As I mentioned previously in the *'Changes'* section and the Teespring story – SEO should also only ever be a **part** of a strategy. Much in the way a platform like Facebook can change their terms of service and render an entire lead generating mechanism obsolete – the same can be said for Googles algorithmic changes.

Much has been mentioned about being penalised for being Black Hat – but that's not always the case. As mentioned, Google is refining it's algorithm all the time, and if something that once had you on the first page is given less weight – you may end up on page two.

As the saying goes:

> *"If you want to hide a dead body, put it on page 2 of Google!"*

…because nobody's looking there.

If you've based your entire lead generation strategy around users searching for your product or service on Google – you're sitting on a potential ticking time bomb, as it's based on something that's mostly out of your control. More often than not an SEO professional can find out what the thing you need to change to accommodate the new algorithm, but by that time it could be too late.

SEO, particularly for a new business, is a slow burn. It can take many months to rank your website for terms that actually impact your business.

SEO needs to be a lifestyle choice – not a diet.

You have to make it part of your business and allow the passage of time to gradually take you where you want to be. The more content you create - the more backlinks you will garner over time and the more keywords you will rank - like a compound effect.

Like I mentioned in the *'Authority'* section earlier – the better quality content you create, the more traffic you will get. When Google sees you are getting lots of traffic and sees your visitors are staying to consume, they will position you as an authority in your field, compared to your competition - be that in your street, your town, your city, your country or even the world.

Build it up gradually with good quality content.

PPC

(Pay Per Click)

Typically, when someone mentions PPC - they're referring to Google Ads. It does what the name suggests – you pay every time someone clicks your link, or advert.

Google Ads come in many different forms. When you do a Google search, you'll see the top 10 results as explained in the previous section. These are called the Organic Results. Organic because they are the *'natural'* results of the search engines algorithm - but you'll also see ads at the very top before these organic results, and after. These ads are paid for by the company to be there (at time of writing you'll see a green box that says *'Ad'* somewhere on it).

However, Google can also have your ads placed on various websites that are sometimes relevant to your industry. It could just be a text, or it could be an image. Even websites that have no relevance to your business have blank ad space that's filled by the Retargeting that was mentioned earlier – meaning the ads are tailored for every individual person based on their browsing activity.

What's great about PPC?

- It's free until someone clicks on a link, so you only pay when someone clicks your ad.
- It's a great way to get on to the first page of Google while you build up your SEO.
- You can split test many different combinations of imagery, sales copy, landing pages and target audience – honing your ads to find what gets the best response. Then, with this information you can not only have better PPC ads – you can implement those findings across all of your ads on all of your platforms.
- You can set a daily budget, so you never go over what you intend to spend. In simple terms, if you set a daily budget of £4 and your keyword cost is 50p per click – after 8 clicks that day Google will stop showing

your ad.

- Once you get more sophisticated with your Google Ads use, you can use their conversion tracking software to help discover the exact amount of sales you have from your PPC efforts. From what specific ad your customer came from to the process they went through before buying, the data tells you, rather than having to ask each customer how they found you (particularly useful if you sell to a lot of customers or never physically speak to them).

There's not many downsides, other than most searchers prefer to click the organic traffic – but if you're only paying when someone **does** click, then it's no big deal. Another pitfall you can get into is if your product doesn't have a high enough mark-up. For example:

- Your gift box sells for £30, and you're being charged £1 per click by Google, and you average 40 clicks before you get a sale – then you're into -£10 before you even count your own costs to make the product.
- Your tech product sells for £300 and you're being charged £2 per click by Google (because it's in a more competitive space), and you still average 40 clicks before you get a sale. That's £80 in ads per £300 sale, minus your costs.
- Your engineering equipment sells for £30,000 and you're being charged £4 per click by Google (more competitive again), still 40 clicks per sale. Now it costs you £160 to get a £30k sale.
- Your online course or digital product is £900 and it costs the same £160 per sale, but because it's a digital product that has virtually no overheads other than a website and your time to initially create the product and monitor your ads, then it's nearly 100% profit. You're basically trading £160 for £900 each time.

Make sure the Return On Investment (ROI) is worthwhile on the ad spend vs what the product or service costs you. The only exception to this is knowing your customer lifetime value (CLV) as I mentioned before, and if you're willing to have a loss leader on the original sale due to the upsell or future sales those customers make.

The Cost Per Click (CPC) is determined by the competition in the industry and the location. There is no limit to the number of keywords you can rank for, often in the hundreds and even thousands. Some businesses deliberately show ads for the names of their competitors to poach business when a user searches for a particular company name. You can also set the parameters of your ad to only appear to searchers in a particular country, state, region or even town.

At time of writing, on the top of a Google search there is room for 4 ads before it moves on to the organic results and 3-Pack. The order of those 4 ads is determined by each businesses max bid on their CPC. If you set all your keywords to the minimum bid, you'll for sure appear somewhere, but you'll be at the bottom of the paid ads on the page.

Not always a bad thing.

I tend to set a cheaper CPC but overcome my client's position by having better sales copy that entices searchers to click on my ads instead - even if they're not at the top.

You are also ranked higher in the ads if your ads have proven to be more successful with searchers than others. Basically, if you have your audience targeting right, your sales copy enticing and landing page proven useful and relevant – Google will reward you with better positioning. This may seem counter-intuitive for a business like Google to charge you less, the more successful your ads are performing, but remember, as is the same with SEO:

Google's number 1 objective, above all else is to provide the best, most accurate experience for it's searchers. This is their reputation and why 90% of the world's searches are on Google.

Always keep that in mind when you're using SEO or Google Ads – if you focus on helping the searcher, you're also improving your position with Google as a by-product.

With a lot of paid advertising it's an important note that you can reach critical mass, a sort of glass ceiling for your ads. If you spend £1,000 on ads and that nets you £10,000 in sales – that doesn't necessarily mean if you spend £10,000 on ads that you'll get £100,000 in sales.

To oversimplify it: Imagine you trimmed specialist interiors for Range Rovers, and you set the ad demographic to only the town that your workshop is based. The town has a population of 1,000 and 10 of them have Range Rovers. Even assuming all of those 10 are interested in your product, once your ads hits those 10 people and they buy either in that moment or through Retargeting – you've reached that glass ceiling. You can't double your investment and get 20 people, because they don't exist.

It's important to have your keywords going to the appropriate pages. This can be done in bulk, but make sure each keyword goes to the corresponding page, not your homepage (unless your homepage is the page with the information on that keyword). Either a page, or better yet – a case study. As mentioned before - make sure your particular services have their own dedicated pages on your website so when a user clicks an ad for that keyword it goes directly to that page.

Another good strategy is using the keywords in your PPC campaign that Google suggests to you, seeing the search volume for them and then incorporating that into your SEO strategy.

You won't know if PPC will work until you try, look at the figures and adjust accordingly. It's part of the 80/20 rule where it might not be so fruitful, but it could be part of that 20% that makes 80% of the profit!

Start with knowing the result you want, like:

- Encouraging your potential customers to call you.
- Encouraging them to buy on your online store.
- Encouraging them to physically come into your store.
- Promoting a new product.
- Drive new traffic to your website that your pixel gathers for Retargeting.
- Signing up for your newsletter or downloading an eBook.

This determines how you run your campaign.

As I say - your ads should go to a landing page on your website specifically designed to convert potential customers into the result you want. More on landing pages and copy later, but make sure:

- Your call to action is above the fold (immediately visible without having to scroll).
- The page URL is similar to the product (i.e. www.yourwebsite.com/over-50s-life-insurance).
- The page copy and, if relevant, imagery are similar to the ad.

You want to make it as easy as possible for the potential customer to get the result they want, and when they click from an ad to a sales page it needs to read and look similar so they have confidence the ad is indeed what it says it is. The continuity helps build confidence in you massively.

SOCIAL MEDIA

First - you need to be present. It's essential. It's where the audience is. You control the narrative. You can showcase what you do. You can humanise what you do. You can handle objections or complaints.

But if you're going to be present then you need to understand that this is **reflective** of your business, so it has to be compelling, interesting, useful, educational content that is at least as good as you are at whatever it is you do, and it can't stagnate. Much like a website and often more so – it's the shop window into your business and despite being entirely on the internet - it should be used to humanise you.

Be authentic and be the real you.

It's how to have a more honest conversation with your clients because they have the protection of the screen (a lot easier to be critical when not face to face).

It's how you showcase what your customers are saying about you in a good way and flipping something bad that's said by making it right (or explaining your side), also known as Reputation Management.

It's how you establish yourself as an authority in your space. Which might be: The best Garage in your neighbourhood, or city, or country, or even beyond. Teaming up with similar companies or the same kind of companies to piggyback off each other's success and audience.

It's how you give VALUE. Real value before you even try to make a sale. Famous fitness coach Joe Wicks posted 20,000 tweets before he ever monetised his audience. Hard work and delivering real value built his empire. He is not special. You can do the same, but you have to be willing to put in the work. Don't think you'll post and suddenly get a ton of traffic. Give more value than you ever thought necessary.

You must dig in and really work at it - there's no overnight success.

Posting regularly on social media is essential, but it's incredibly hard – almost impossible for most business owners to create original content, say, twice a day, given time constraints. Not only this but most industries don't have the daily subject matter for it. This means you might need to supplement your posting with industry content. Positioning yourself as an expert, not only with your own content but showing that you have your finger on the pulse everywhere across your industry to build goodwill.

Think about everything that's involved in your business, day to day that you take for granted:

- Sections of your website that give an insight into your business or services.
- Tell everyone your latest news: What you're doing or where you are that day, what accreditations you or your staff are working towards or have achieved.
- Write an industry related blog post.
- Talk about clients you're working with.
- Case studies you've built
- Reviews you've had.
- If you have a product list, you can feature individual ones each day.
- If your business is more fun than serious – use funny videos and memes.
- Calls to action, whether that's to buy, to contact you, to visit a specific page of your website, to attend your event, to join your group…

…and so on. The more you post the more engagement you get, the bigger your social platforms grow and the bigger reach you have.

The calls to action one is important because once you gain traction on your platforms they should be normalised. Not in a douche who's seen Glengarry Glen Ross too many times kind of way:

> *"A-B-C.*
> *A - Always, B - Be, C - Closing.*
> *Always be closing."*
> - Blake, Glengarry Glen Ross

No. However it might seem unfair, but if you own a brand and suddenly start asking for calls to action when you didn't before, even if you've been providing good value for years until that point – it can switch your audience off. Make sure your audience are used to it. Give way more value in posts than calls to action, though. Just make sure they're in there.

When it comes to selling, use social media to:

- Encourage existing customers to buy again.
- Encourage existing customers to spend more when they do buy.
- Encourage existing customers to recommend you to their friends, family and colleagues.
- Direct potential new customers into your sales funnel.

Get creative with your social media, including researching what works in your particular industry. Some of the best content, though, comes from business owners doing something completely new, or at least bucking a trend. Is your subject matter really dry? Can you make it more interesting on some of the more *'relaxed'* platforms and open yourself up to a whole new audience to which you have the entire market share? Similarly – can you take something that someone would typically rolls their eyes at and intellectualise it; making them think? Being unique is hard when it's not for uniques sake – but when it works it's captivating, explodes your reach and has everyone wanting to do an interview with you.

Social media in the last few years has been an incredible platform for streaming live content. Never in any other situation in history has a business been able to reach so many people with so much sincere content. Live streaming allows you to give your viewers a truly honest insight into your business – and they **love** it. The authenticity of live streaming cannot be underestimated – like having your own live TV channel. If you have a genuinely good, ethical business that serves its customers well and believes in its product – you have nothing to fear.

There's new live streaming businesses and apps coming out all of the time, but a few of the more current, popular examples are:

- Facebook Live.
- Instagram Stories / Instagram TV (IGTV).
- YouTube Live.
- Snapchat.

What should you be doing live broadcasts on?

- Talking about your products or services or showing them in action.
- Product development.
- *'Behind the scenes'.*
- An insight into your life, particularly if it's relevant to your business or personal brand.
- Charity work you're doing.
- Special guests.
- Interviews.
- An event you're holding.
- Helping customers with their work.
- Tutorials.

- *"Ask Me Anything".*
- Troubleshooting.
- Create a 'series'.
- Handle objections.
- Clear up any (particularly false) bad press.
- Motivation.
- Real-time information for fast-paced businesses.

When running a clients' social media, it typically falls into supplementing the clients own post with curated content such as industry related news, listing products or services from their website, repurposing reviews into images and so on – but the client needs trained on their own posting. They should understand that their own content is invaluable once they get good at understanding how to post it effectively.

Nobody knows your business as good as you.

OK, now it's time to get platform specific…

FACEBOOK

Facebook is the world's biggest social platform, so is it likely your customers are on there? From experience, as a general rule of thumb the only thing hard to sell on there is big ticket items for high net worth individuals:

A) Because big ticket items tend to require a bit more trust than an ad on one of the more relaxed social platforms.

B) Because high net worth individuals aren't typically dicking about on Facebook like the rest of us peasants, due to their drive and work ethic (…and sociopathic tendencies).

Remember though, that rules of thumb are made to be broken. Big ticket items alone can be sold on Facebook if it's, say, cosmetic dentistry. Also, you might not sell to the high net worth individual in that moment but what if it's just a retargeting ad that keeps your product or service in their mind when they've already visited your website.

…or to hell with rules (even of thumb) - your ad might be so good, your sales copy so exemplary that you manage to get sales anyway.

Remember what I said about why I never specialised or niched down to one service – if I'd just worked with Facebook, any client where that platform didn't fit their demographic or selling strategy would have to go with someone else. This ensured I covered all skills and all platforms – you should do the same in marketing your business. Be sure to cover it, but manage your expectations depending on your business.

When it comes to Facebook you must remember what I said previously – post regularly. Almost as much as possible without diluting the quality. Most of my clients are posting 2 or 3 times per day. You might need even more. Use the strategies mentioned in the social media section previously to populate your Facebook with a mixture of your own and industry related content.

Get creative, too. A good example would be to create a private Facebook group for your existing customers where you can give tips and they can ask questions. This could be an exercise in you delivering more value to your customers and also keeping you in their mind. This way you can more directly advertise to them for more business or have them recommend you to their friends, family or others in their industry. Alternatively, you could even charge customers to be in the group, where they get more face time with you or have questions answered.

Reviews. Ask for reviews. Always be requesting reviews.

Reviews are the biggest social proof you can ask for, and most businesses don't have a strategy to ask for them. How you ask will be dependent on your industry.

My builder client communicates via phone calls and texts with each client and can complete multiple jobs in a day. After each job he sends a text to each client thanking them for their business and a link to the reviews section on his Facebook page, along with a link to his Google listing reviews (there are tools where you can get the direct link to this, rather than asking to client to search for you).

Once he implemented this, his reviews soared. He went from virtually none to hundreds in just one year.

Every time someone writes a review on his Facebook, he responds with a thank you message and a link to his Google review, in the hope his customer reviews on there also. Now, how does it look when someone visits his Facebook page organically or sees one of his ads and clicks through? Literally hundreds of positive reviews proving his company is as good as he says it is.

The Google reviews help massively with his organic SEO, with Google ranking him higher as a result of the social proof. His Facebook reviews also help with this in a more indirect way, with Google seeing that his company is spoken of highly on there.

Good reviews are also essentially important in drowning out negative reviews. Not to hide them, but to give a more accurate representation of his real life feedback. The problem being - customers typically only leave a review off their own back when they are dissatisfied and need to vent, or want to purposefully harm the businesses reputation.

The rest need actively encouraged or reminded.

My orthodontist client asks for a review there and then after a treatment. Meaning the customer gets out their phone and leaves an honest review. Good or bad he gives them something free in return (at time of writing it's currently a few months supply of cleaner for the braces they've just had fitted). Once his staff were trained to ask and shown how to get to the review section of the Facebook app – that was it.

My jeweller client sends these as part of his thank you email, along with his Trust Pilot and Yell links. There are many ways to ask for your reviews, and as I say they'll depend on your industry and how you typically communicate with your clients.

Be sure you're asking across all of your platforms including Trip Advisor if you are a travel destination, Check-A-Trade if you are a tradesman - and so on with whatever review platform is relevant to your industry and country.

TWITTER

Twitter has a massive user base – it's mostly good for virtue signalling and *'how can I make **your** thing about **me**?'*.

Only joking…

Not really.

…but from a business point of view Twitter can be great. You can get right into local conversations by running a search for, say:

"<insert your business or service> <insert town, city or country>"

…or even better – leave out the town, city or country if you can service anywhere.

Change it from *'Top'* to *'Latest'* and look through the most recent conversations and see if you could message anyone to solve their issue.

If you are a custom jeweller, then no doubt you make wedding rings that you can ship anywhere. For 10 minutes a day you could search twitter for:

"got engaged"

"getting married"

You could tweet back to the ones that are real people announcing their news saying you have a special offer running on bespoke wedding rings to make their day extra special.

Like I say:

- 10 minutes.
- Every day.

- Test different reply styles, offers and messages.
- Get your first sale.
- Now you've proven that style works, up it to 20 minutes per day.
- Get so good at finding the right ones you get more and more sales.
- You're now doing an hour a day because it's so lucrative.
- Now either rinse – lather – repeat and make hay while the sun shines or get it down to an exact science and train a staff member, your partner, an outsourcer to do it (although in this particular instance it probably needs someone that knows you and your business well).

You can also use the same search to get real time information about what people are saying about your industry:

- What the public like about it.
- What pisses them off.
- What they're saying about your competitors.
- What they're saying about **you**!
- What your competition is doing so well that you can then replicate.

You can wade in on the conversation and discuss, help, debate and position yourself as an expert or an authority in your industry or niche. Alternatively, you can be a quiet observer and learn.

You also don't have to be *'friends'* or *'connected'* with people like you do in other platforms, so particularly if you are more B2B you can seek out individuals (or owners, partners, managers) and companies and start getting involved in the conversations that they are having. A seamless way to get involved in a dialog without a hard-sell.

Twitter also has a feed like most other social platforms which you can use to put out information, news and anything else you would on the other platforms. The only drawback to posting is, at time of writing it's limited to 280 characters (up from 140 historically). It's also the birthplace of hashtags - so the same principals you'll learn about hashtags in the Instagram section should be applied here also.

Be sure to constantly *'like'* tweets that are relevant in your industry – both from the public or other businesses if you're B2B. Liked tweets are seen by the potential customer / connection and they'll look at your profile (that you've surely honed as a sales page in its own right) or at least they'll hopefully follow you. You can do this manually if you know industry people or you can search tweets for keywords or hashtags that would be relevant in your industry or niche.

You can also create lists to categorise the accounts you follow. This is helpful as a ready-made list you can visit when you want to focus on a particular group – but it also works to get you noticed as the account you put in the list gets an alert that you put them in the list and the name of that list, thus exposing them to you.

Twitter allows you to pin 1 tweet of yours to the top on your profile, meaning regardless of posts you make after it – that post will still remain at the top. This could be your best ever tweet, the most popular tweet you've ever made or it could be a link to your email subscription, eBook, or a particular sales page or case study you always want to show off and be one of the first things users see when they visit your profile. Twitter also lets you customise your pinned tweet to be more of a button to help it stand out more and boost engagement.

INSTAGRAM

Instagram is the only social platform that I enjoy posting on personally. It doesn't have the noise and drama of Twitter, it doesn't have judgement of Facebook and it's mostly just posting a quick image or video, unlike going all-in on YouTube.

I post bits of my life that my friends and family like, and (from my own personal experience at least) away from jealousy and the:

"Oh, you're just trying to make your life look good!"

...because that's what Instagram is usually about – it's casual and cool. I don't want to bore or bother people with my problems. If I did, I'd talk to an actual close human being, face-to-face, with a real conversation, or at worst by phone call. I don't need social media to validate my existence or to prop up my difficult days – you shouldn't either.

Now, back to business. Instagram is epic for business. Why? The sheer amount of scope you have to reach who you want to reach. It allows you to create a really attractive *'shop window'* of your product or service, and as we'll discuss later – cheap (at time of writing at least) for ads.

Instagram is constantly evolving, too. It rolls out new services regularly that always have a business spin on how to generate leads or monetise it. It even has cool little nuggets that marketers discover - for example, at time of writing a good technique is posting your images with a portrait (vertical) crop - meaning when it appears on your followers feed you've got more screen real estate!

Start, as always, with filling out your profile. Instagram's profile section is pretty good. It allows you plenty of characters to convey your message, allows hashtags in the bio to help others find you, lets you use emoji's and it gives you a link to your website (which can be anything). Fill it out with whatever you want.

Remember to link it with your Facebook business page so your business title appears automatically. Make your name something searchable – for example my username is *'@graeme_lawson'* but instead of my actual name I've put *'Marketing & Business Growth'*, and Facebook's categorised title for me is *'Business Consultant'* (rather than *'Misanthropic Rockstar'* – but you pick your battles).

Give your profile some personality, humanise you or your business. Then at the end of the bio, immediately before your hyperlink – give context for that hyperlink. If you're just creating your profile now, you can put *'To learn more, click below'*, but change it to something better later. Like a link to your email opt in or eBook, your latest blog post, or the section of your website that has the product or service you most want to sell, or the Amazon link to your new Get Unemployed book...

When you post – be sure to utilise hashtags. This is the best way to break through from just your own followers. A hashtag is a keyword that other people can search for and see the feed of every post with that tag. It looks like a hash # (or *'number'*) followed by the text. So #sunset will be a bunch of sunsets posted by users. If you post a picture of a kitchen you've redesigned with the hashtags: #kitchen #newkitchen #redesignedkitchen #kitchenmakeover #customkitchen #kitchensmanchester #plumbing etc. – basically everything relevant in the picture.

In fact, I just tried it there with #kitchen. It gives you a bunch of suggestions with the popularity of that hashtag – the top in this instance being #kitchendesign with nearly 4 million posts! So, use the data Instagram effortlessly gives you and make sure you have the top hashtags pertaining to your image in there. This means when someone searches that hashtag – your one will come up.

Think of obscure ones that might have low popularity also, though. What might get lost in a sea of popular ones – when a potential customer is looking for something very specific and you have hashtagged it, and the post is good – you'll likely get the sale.

If you want to find out what posts get the most engagement, canvass what's working in other accounts in your industry. If certain posts have many more thousands of likes than their account average, then build your content around those posts. Do not copy the post exactly but replicate the subject matter - if you can prove by abnormal amounts of likes and comments on particular posts on accounts then that subject matter is obviously popular with that industries audience. Rinse, lather, repeat.

It's great for local selling. You can search for your town, city, country – however wide or deep you want to go - then hit the *'Places'* tab. Here it'll give you the most popular photos for people that have tagged themselves in that location. This is good as they'll be the most popular, because typically they'll have the most engagement – and they'll typically have the most engagement because they have a lot of followers – and if they have a lot of followers, they might have a good reach in the area. As I've mentioned previously – followers and engagement might mean nothing if people aren't buying, but these people are the *'Top'* posts because they

are actually getting the engagement.

Anyway, post genuine comments on these images – sincere comments that are relevant to the account holders post. The people that use bots for this – you see them coming a mile away and it's a huge turn-off. Be real and put in the time and effort to post unique comments on all the relevant top posts. Then switch it from *'Top'* to *'Recent'* and go through the recent ones, manually, for 10 minutes a day.

Then switch it up and target relevant hashtags, local or otherwise and do the same. When you do a search for what you think might be the main hashtag – Instagram gives you a bunch of suggested hashtags that are popular and relevant to the one you've just put in, giving you further scope to explore.

This is huge and a real power that every Instagram user has. Set the time aside to do it because if you want to pay an agency to do it – it's going to cost. You can literally do this yourself, for 10, 20, 30 minutes before you go to bed. You could do it for 1 hour a day. Do you know how much your business would benefit if you did this for an hour every day? Do you know how much 30 hours a month would cost you to pay an agency? The power is literally in your hands.

Use this technique and you'll gain followers. The people your targeting will visit your profile and you'll have that optimised to convert in whatever way you want.

To take this further - you could private message those accounts. Again, I hope this goes without saying, but you should **not** be in someone's inbox without good reason. Whatever you propose must be infinitely in their favour.

In fact, offering something completely for free is not unreasonable if they have a large following. Why not offer those with big following in your city free personal training for a month, free teeth whitening, free SEO for a month like I did. You could offer a genuine celebrity a free bathroom, a chauffeur drive or a free custom made ring – whatever your business is and whatever would genuinely give them something of substance. You are not offering a *'Free IT Audit'* - that is you obviously looking to backdoor into their business. It has to be something that if they do nothing else, they get to have whatever the *'thing'* is that's massively in their favour.

You could openly ask for a review or a shout-out for it if you're scared they'll just take it and run, or you could just do it and let reciprocity take its course. This is not being a Busy Fool. This is fast tracking you to exposure that would take a long time, likely years, to typically build from a standing start.

Another good strategy is encouraging users to tag their friends. Anything from saying:

"Tag a friend who needs this!"

182

"Tag a friend who would like this!"

"Tag a friend who does this!"

In your image description, to provoke engagement, you could even run a competition where tagging a friend enters them into a draw – then say you can't tag yourself, but your friend can tag you back! This improves your reach greatly and is also a great strategy for most social platforms. Also, when someone buys your product or service - ask them to take a picture and tag you. You can even run a competition between those that do that in each week or month, depending on your frequency.

If you post in your feed with hashtags to build your audience, you use *'Stories'* to nurture them. Stories are the time-sensitive posts that appear at the top of the app. Time-sensitive because they automatically delete themselves after 24 hours. They can be pictures, videos, animations …just about anything. You can scribble over them, put text, emoji's or gifs over them.

Stories are now more popular than the feed itself. You'll know this is true if you use Instagram already, because of the creepy fucks that watch all of your stories but never like your posts.

They can be anything, but the clue is in the name – tell a **story**. Have it make sense in continuity. It can be personal to humanise you or business to give an insight into the inner workings of your company.

It can also be used for calls to action. You'll need 10,000 followers to get the *'Swipe Up'* feature, but you can circumvent this with gifs and polls. In the poll example you could ask if someone wants to buy, say, your new Get Unemployed book and have the poll say Yes or No. You'll see the ones that say yes, and you can private message them directly.

Encouraging someone to take action away from your feed and into your private messages or another post **is a must**. There are various workarounds for different obstacles, but I'll bet it'll change again soon – so don't get hung up on it.

Instagram Live and IGTV should also be utilised but not to be confused as the same thing.

Live is like a longer version of what is typically a Story, and of course – you film live. They are the same as Stories in that they disappear after 24 hours. This is good for creating a buzz. It's similar to the social media general list I posted previously:

- If you have a new product coming out.
- *'Behind the scenes'* footage.
- An insight into your life.
- Special guests you've got coming on your IGTV, YouTube, Facebook

Live or podcast.
- A teaser about an event.
- Helping customers with their work.
- A quick tutorial.
- Troubleshooting.
- Answering a question.
- Handling objections.
- Clear up any (particularly false) bad press.
- Motivation.
- Real-time information for fast-paced businesses.

You can also engage with your viewers in real time. Viewers can communicate with you, make comments and ask questions that you could answer right there on the video …or you can turn them off.

IGTV is more like a YouTube channel, arguably for the more casual or *'trendy'* publisher (I got way more douche-chills typing that than you did reading it, trust me). This can be for videos up to 10 minutes (and 60 minutes if you get to that 10,000 followers count again). It's like having your own TV show – and you can edit your videos before they go out. You can post:

- Interviews.
- *'How To'* videos.
- A weekly or monthly show as a *'round up'*.
- Also, longer versions of most of the of the other list above.

"We've come to the end of the Instagram section, Graeme - why haven't you talked about Influencers?"

…because they're mostly dicks.

However, you are posting on Instagram, remember - post often. More posts mean more engagement, more engagement means more people in those engaging's sphere having your content recommended to them. Always make sure your content is entertaining or educational.

Also, did I mention that Instagram stories are really cheap right now for paid ads? More on that later…

PINTEREST

Typically, good when targeting women, food, fashion, travel, beauty and design – Pinterest is a search engine for images that then link to where they actually exist on a certain website. However, chances are your audience is almost everywhere, so don't discount Pinterest as only for housewives and designers.

Pinterest works by users curating *'boards'* of images. Those images, as I say, hotlink directly to a source - preferably your website! If you have images on your website you should be embedding them into Pinterest, meaning when anyone clicks that pin (image) it will take them to your website. If one of your pins takes off with many users adding it to their own board – the link still goes to your website, giving you a potentially massive reach.

A quick and easy way to do this is to have a Pinterest plugin on your website. As long as you're logged into Pinterest on your web browser you can click the Pinterest button when you hover over your own website image and distribute it to your appropriate board - easy! You can even use their own Pin Scheduler if you have a business account where you can do all the work at once, but stagger your pins and make it look more natural.

Delving deeper? Be specific in your image descriptions – as detailed as possible. Pinterest needs to know what an image is so it can deliver it to its searchers accordingly. Most users don't do this, particularly casual consumers - so when you do it you get a massive advantage over them.

You should have a board for each of your services, or demographics, or …it's going to depend entirely on your own business. I suggest either using common sense or googling the best way to segment your boards for your industry. Each of your boards should have an attractive board cover – a good image with perhaps a border or text on it to differentiate you from the rest. Show visiting users that your profile is professional and an authority in your niche. Test different styles and use the analytics to gauge the response. Find out what works and do more of that, again with the 80/20 rule. Name your boards exactly the same as the most popular keywords (remember the trick of starting to type in the search bar and looking for what Pinterest tries to auto-fill it with).

Go deeper again and start contributing to Group Boards. These are community boards like groups on Facebook or LinkedIn where several members join to enjoy the pins posted by the Group Collaborators. You can then join a group and ask the owner if you can become a collaborator. There are different ways to do this, some more relaxed where you can just click *'Add Me'* but typically in the more popular ones with the bigger reach you have to contact the group owners and they'll manually check your profile to see if you fit the bill.

To get traffic from Pinterest, as with everything you need to test what works, finding the best pins and posting them often. It won't blow up overnight, but a continued strategy will have a compound effect and you'll be building up website views just by linking pictures you've already posted on your website!

LINKEDIN

LinkedIn is almost the opposite of most social platforms. Facebook, Instagram, Twitter, Pinterest and so on are far more relaxed and considered places to digitally *'hang out'*. LinkedIn has a reputation for being this wooden, corporate, fountain pens and 3-piece-suits place where creative dreams go to die.

This couldn't be further from the truth.

As with all platforms it's what you make of it and how you design your corner of it. What if you dismiss it entirely but it turns out to be where you get most of your best customers? Yes, it's more expensive to advertise, but maybe as I illustrated in a previous section – it's where your better, higher paying clients sign up for your product or service?

LinkedIn is mostly B2B, this is undisputed – but it opens up a whole world of connections and targeting to find the **right** people for you and your niche.

First of all – have a fully completed profile. The default LinkedIn alert system actually does a pretty good job of bugging you into finishing it properly. Take the time to do it because it's essential for a few things:

- Anyone that does research into you finds your LinkedIn page and it's packed full of useful information. Your LinkedIn account, rightly or wrongly like anything else, is a direct reflection on you and your business. Half-filled in account with little information? Half-baked business with little substance. Treat it like your website – a shop window into you and your business.

- If someone randomly lands on your profile you have an opportunity to convert a cold lead.

- From a technical point of view, a fully completed profile would link out to your website. As we've learned with SEO – it's essential to have the keywords you're targeting on pages that link to your website.

Next up is groups. Join groups that are relevant to your industry or services. Once you're in those groups you can contribute and be genuinely helpful. By doing so you position yourself as an expert or even thought leader in those groups. From there you'll either have members contacting you privately about further help, or you could even put it out there that you welcome private help. Those who are members of the same group can message each other from there (normally you would need to be mutually connected) so you have a direct line into a potential customers' inbox. You now have information into both:

- Other people in your industry and learning what they do well.

- Your potential customers, what their true pain points are and what kind of language they use to articulate it, that you can then implement into your sales copy.

Groups often have hundreds or even thousands of members. You can use the search function within the group to segment them based on the likes of their location or specific job title.

Going deeper? You could contact the group owner(s) and offer them a fee (or a cut) to promote your services to their audience. There's also an announcement feature group owners have that can be utilised in this instance.

What about creating your own group that you can manage and have full control over? You can exclusively 'sponsor' the group and have sole marketing autonomy over it or you can pick the sponsors and have them pay you. At that stage you will need to have created the worthy asset worth renting out. This is the only downside starting from scratch but if you're willing to take the time over the weeks, months and years to build it – you could have an incredible asset to which you control. What better way to establish yourself as an authority on a subject than an owner of a big LinkedIn group on the industry or service?

LinkedIn is also a publishing platform. You can post articles you write on there. Be careful about duplicate content with articles that you post on your own website. If I'm going to post something to both, I make sure it's on my own website for a month before I post the same to anywhere else. This allows plenty of time for Google to index it first on your website and know that is the original source – otherwise it could look like you stole it from LinkedIn.

Providing you're logged into LinkedIn on your web browser you can put a social sharing plugin on your website (you should probably have one of these anyway). When you click on your own *'LinkedIn Share'* on that plugin for a blog you've written it'll ask you where on LinkedIn you want to distribute it – this way you can quickly share it to multiple groups you are a member of. This has both a time advantage and, rather than link someone to your LinkedIn article – you're feeding them directly to your website.

They might have a look around in that case, and who knows…

In the same way you'd share something to your existing audience - you now have the additional potential reach of all the members of those groups you're a member of added together! Not only this but it's also significantly more targeted. Posting something on, say, your personal social profile only has a certain amount of people interested from a targeting point of view. With groups the target market is honed.

A link to your website, giving a bunch of really useful information to your exact target market.

You're giving value, positioning yourself as an expert and authority in your industry or niche.

LinkedIn has a great system where it tells you how many degrees of separation you are from another person. If you know your client demographic and therefore the type of person you would like an introduction to – you can ask the mutual friend to introduce you.

Like the traditional ways of doing business – your middle man mutual friend acts as a buffer and gives you credibility over a cold contact. Even if you don't want to give that mutual connection the hassle of putting it together you could even just ask the person to connect and just mention the mutual friend *"<mutual connection> suggested we connect"*. Always get the mutual connections permission first (I feel like this should go without saying, but you never know).

Be sure to take time out every week whenever you can to use these strategies. They really work. As with all strategies - take a little longer and nurture users and connection before you sell them. They are people too and want to feel a real connection before you beat them over the head with your offer. When it comes the time to promote that offer to them – be sure to provide incredible value, making your offer a no brainer. They've allowed you in – don't abuse it.

YOUTUBE

YouTube is the social platform I spend most of my time on. Easily. It has an unfathomable amount of information stored, with over 300 hours uploaded every single minute.

There is now no excuse for not knowing how to do or achieve just about anything.

I'm not alone. Over 70% of adults use YouTube, and with the 18 to 24 age demographic it's over 90%! More than half the population watch more online video than they do regular TV, with the average mobile session being over 40 minutes. The shift is no longer happening. It's happened. It's done. So how have businesses responded?

Less than 10% of small businesses use YouTube.

I never really thought about YouTube as a business model until I started watching Gary Vaynerchuk on Wine Library TV. I don't get hipster about much, but I was definitely watching Gary (now probably better known as *'Gary V' or 'Vee'*) before he got really big, probably around 2008.

Gary's story is incredible.
...or more accurately: Gary's personality *'type'* is incredible.

He has a work ethic and love for the game that typically only billionaires have. He's a psychologists' wet dream, but he understands that most people aren't cut from the same cloth and want more of a balance in life. He makes sacrifices I wouldn't, but he's the type of trailblazer you should learn from.

He got involved in a wine selling business his very poor, immigrant dad grew from nothing into a 3 million dollars per year business. After Gary switched the narrative from *'wine discount'* to *'wine library'* and utilised internet ads in the way nobody really was doing at the time, he grew the business from $3,000,000 to $60,000,000 in a few short years.

What's that got to do with YouTube? Well, Gary gets a lot of things right, including investing in Facebook, Twitter and Snapchat early. In fact, investing in such a way, he could've cashed in his chips and sat on the beach sipping cocktails with his family, many times over, a long time ago. He also gets some things wrong, but as we discussed in the Mindset section, his willingness to have a mixture of both and not care about those losses is why he succeeds.

YouTube was a big deal for Gary. He was convinced online video was the next big thing and would have a kind of growth few would predict. So, he doubled down on the show he created called Wine Library TV and started both educating people about wine in a real way and taking the piss out of the snobbery in the industry. A formerly disinterested, younger, working class drinking audience were now interested. When I say *'now'* I don't mean right away:

Gary started his YouTube show Wine Library TV in 2006. He stopped 5 years later on episode 1,000...

Are you getting it yet? The dedication and the persistence often needed to achieve what you want to achieve. You will have success if you apply yourself relentlessly – no exceptions.

I didn't even drink wine, but watching Gary literally lick a rock and compare it to the taste he was getting from a particular red was hilarious and genuinely engaging, while always sharing with us his dream (and plan) of one day owning the New York Jets.

At first, nobody was watching. This is a guy who'd 20X'd his dads' business doing videos online that nobody was watching. It was hundreds of shows until he gathered momentum in the wild west that was early YouTube.

When he released his first book *'Crush It'* in 2009 I couldn't believe what I was reading. It was like a seismic shift in the way people did business that I could understand, be part of and use to reach an almost unlimited audience.

Gary went on to start his own digital agency focussing on social media, which is now one of the biggest in the world. He also gets paid $75,000 minimum to speak at events.

He built almost all of his online reputation on YouTube, and more broadly, video in general.

Sitting thinking about all that you can do on the platform is incredibly exciting. You have access to several devices that can record in real time and upload in minutes. It's liberating!

...until it comes to actually filming.

Rabbit in the headlights much? Saying you want to do it, getting excited about it then actually being faced with talking on camera, editing it and putting it out there that your family, friends, colleagues, classmates and so on can see can be painfully difficult. I mean, it shouldn't be – but for most it's a fact of life that only the dedicated get over.

I wanted to start my own car show back in 2009 while those sorts of things were still gathering momentum on YouTube, but fear of failure stopped me many times. I even practiced filming it, overthought it and never dared publish anything.

Everything anyone ever posts first time is garbage. Like I said earlier in the book - you have to start with what is crap, learn from your mistakes and what your audience wants and modify it accordingly, getting better and better. I never did it and it was infuriating looking at guys that started a show around the same time I was thinking about doing it - building their channels, with many channel owners in their own countries like the UK, US, Germany, Netherlands being invited by networks to present on actual TV shows!

Who knows where my now fictitious car channel would be if I'd pushed through the fear of failure and understood that you need to be willing to have everyone see your shit product before it becomes a good one?

If I wanted to create a car channel (although it'd probably now be a motorbike channel!) these days - I'd just go ahead and do it. Worry wouldn't come into it. Sometimes not only do you grow from trial and error, failure and success – you learn from regret. I don't regret not going for it, but I'd be lying if I said I wasn't intrigued about what would have happened had I pushed through, creating crap until it wasn't crap.

YouTube is also great for business because it's the world's second biggest search engine behind Google. Users are literally searching for your services in the millions.

If you have a smartphone - you have the ability to record your own content and reach that audience. Sometimes the reason content does so well on certain channels is the raw honesty that can come from someone holding up the phone and hitting record.

Quality of production can get as extreme as you want, though. Big cameras, studio quality microphones and advanced lighting setups are there if it ever takes you down that road, but I always advise starting with whatever you can comfortably afford. If that's just your phone with your earbuds with mic attached, then so be it. Your initial videos won't be the best anyway, so it's almost a waste of splashing out or getting into debt on a credit card for a quality production. As I say, if your channel takes you down that road then build up to it.

Without getting into advice on how to film (again, YouTube has an incredible number of videos on the subject), the only bits of advice I will give is:

- Prioritise the audio quality over everything else. Good, clear sound is more important than high quality video. This includes limiting background noise as best you can.

- Make sure there's plenty of light in front of you or your subject (coming from behind the camera filming).

- Being seen is good, particularly if your personality is part of your brand. You can use screencast software to record your screen while you talk, with it having you, earbuds on, in the corner of the screen. You can record your web browser or, say, a PowerPoint presentation while you talk - depending on the subject matter.

The way you break through near the beginning is creating useful, quality content. Get through the awkward starting phase and if you get to this point - viewers will watch your videos from start to finish. YouTube will take notice of this, along with the likes, comments and subscribers you garner and will place you higher when people search. The same principal for your website and SEO is the same with your videos and YouTube's search – YouTube wants to give its searchers the best experience. The best experience is delivering the answer to the search query in the quickest, most consumable and most entertaining way.

When it comes to planning a video, you should start with the result in mind. Who are you helping? What problem are you actually solving? What do you want to cover? The more planning you do beforehand the better the video will be. You don't need a script, as *'riffing'* is absolutely fine if you know the topic well or are good at speaking in general. Sometimes following a script more often than not looks really wooden if you're not a professional – but having a structure is essential.

If you want to start your channel and post about nothing in particular, recording videos on anything that takes your fancy – that's cool, but it's not a business or marketing strategy. Unless you're talking about a scatter gun approach and seeing what little viewers you're getting are responding best to – but that could take a long time. A real business strategy would recognise a need in the market. That might be something that isn't talked about properly anywhere, or it could be that it's being covered poorly in your target area or demographic.

As a business and marketing strategy, start with the goal in mind. Do your research and start typing for industry terms and see what suggestions follow from YouTube's search bar. You can also use the likes of Google Trends to see what's popular in searches.

Plan your video topics, name them, write your descriptions and use your tags according to the data you collect.

Calls to action are essential also. Asking your viewers and community to like, share, subscribe, *'click the bell'* (to alert subscribers when you get a new video), visit your website, join your webinar, download your PDF, donate to your channel at …and so on. You may think these things go without saying, however apathy is a thing in every online audience, so you must promote and provoke action.

Also, be sure to use whatever YouTube's current popups are. There used to be annotations where you could 'overlay' text or links over an uploaded video. These were replaced with information cards that you can have come up at certain points in your video to encourage further engagement. This is why I don't go into great nuts and bolts detail here, because, if this book was written a few years ago the information would be redundant.

The most important are the *'suggested videos'* that come up in the last few seconds of your video. Not ones YouTube decides the viewer might like based on what they've just watched – ones that could send them to another channel. You have the control to encourage your viewer to try another one of your existing videos. This can easily be done in YouTube's video editor.

There are many ways to monetise your YouTube channel. The most obvious is being able to give exposure to your own business, but you can also:

- Encourage viewers into your marketing or sales funnel.
- Visit your website or online store.
- Have a business or multiple businesses sponsor your channel where you give a shout-out in the video with a link to the product or service in your show notes below.
- Visit and buy from another website you earn affiliate commission from. Amazon's is particularly popular and easy to set up.
- Cross-promote with other YouTubers. You guest on my channel, I guest on yours – we then grow as a result of alerting each other's viewers to us (this happens the business world over and is no different to YouTube).

The bulk of YouTubers, from pocket money level commissions to full time jobs, make their money with the platforms Partner Program and YouTube Premium.

YouTube's Partner Program is their own system for helping you monetise your channel, mostly through ads that can appear before, during and after your video and those viewing your channel that have a YouTube Premium subscription. YouTube Premium is a subscription based service that, among other things, removes ads – so when a YouTube Premium viewer looks at your video you get a small cut.

To qualify for YouTube's partner program, at time of writing, your channel needs at least 1,000 subscribers and 4,000 hours of users watching your videos in the past

12 months.

Those numbers in the grand scheme of things are pretty small. When you think about a good rule of thumb being around £2 (or 2.5 USD) earned per 1,000 views – at 1,000 subscribers and 4,000 hours you're not making a lot anyway. The great thing about YouTube numbers is the compound effect of your success. It's typically easier for you to get from 10,000 subscribers to 100,000 than it was to get from zero to 10,000. Plus, if you've niched down with your channels subject matter that means YouTube can tailor your ads better to your audience, meaning you get better clicks on your ads and that £2 per 1,000 views could be significantly more.

YouTube also has a plethora of analytics you can pour over to find out what subject matters in your niche work best, or where users stop watching in a video when you start talking about a particular topic. Like all analytics it's important to study, listen to your audience and go where the market points you.

SOCIAL MEDIA ADVERTISING

How do you fast track your business and get in front of the exact customer demographic you want? Social Ads.

First of all, you need to be willing to spend - and lose the money. There will likely be a degree of testing, sometimes for months before you have a positive ROI. Sometimes you'll knock it out the park right away - but you must be mentally and financially prepared for either scenario.

That being said – start small, regardless of your business size. Don't throw away ad spend if it's not your own money just because you have a lot of it. Test inexpensive campaigns and garner some data. Keep going until you start seeing sales before you ramp it up.

Expectations? Have none.

As I've mentioned previously, you need the right offer to the right people. Particularly to a cold audience the offer must be a no brainer. You have to test the:

- Copy.
- Imagery.
- Offer.
- Audience.

Make sure the first 3 align with the last.

Copy, has to be compelling and draw the reader in. This will vary wildly if you're selling dog walking to the public on Facebook, to dentistry for care homes on LinkedIn. In both instances you're solving a pain point but how you approach both is very different.

In the dog walking example; I used emoji's, guilt and friendship:

- The emoji's are striking and have a friendly tone without cheapening the brand.
- The guilt about leaving your dog in the house all day while you work: *"Is your dog stuck in the house all day, waiting for you to come home?"* with an image of a small, sad dog resting its head on a gate - like he's just watched his owner leave.
- I used Facebook's carousel image, with every image after the sad first one being actual pictures my client took out on her group walks, with the *'gang'* having fun and utter glee on all of the dogs' faces.

The rest of the long form sales copy (more on copywriting later) had:

- Information about the service. The facts.
- Objection handling.
- Social proof.
- Clear calls to action.

In the dentistry for care homes example; I used fear, scarcity and a no-brainer:

- Fear about compliance, given care homes have health obligations to their residents, including oral cancer checks.
- Scarcity because my client regularly reached capacity and had to recruit to grow and maintain the same standard. Care homes had to act quickly or go on a waiting list.
- The no-brainer was that the service was completely managed by my client. The care home simply had to sign off on it, then my client would handle everything: scheduling, treatment (at the care home, so no travel), appointment reminders, paperwork and record keeping.

For **imagery** you'll most likely go for something that shows your product or demonstrates your service – or you can go for a pattern interrupt that shocks the viewer into reading the copy. You can split test several images in your ads to find the ones that perform best. I normally start with 3 then keep the best, add a different 2 and keep working that way until you find the best combination of images. For an accurate representation of what images work best you should keep the copy the same for all images, and again the same when you introduce new ones – otherwise you can't tell what's actually influenced it.

Your **offer** has to be exceptional if you are trying to sell a product or service. Not brand awareness, not watching your video, not getting email subscribers – if you are selling a product or service to a cold audience (even if it's targeted) it has to be a no brainer. Businesses don't go far enough with this. 10% off something is not going to even scratch the surface unless your product costs 100 grand. They think that dangling a meagre carrot is enough to get attention, but all it does is waste money on clicks that don't convert.

It might get someone looking but it's nowhere near strong enough to convert.

Don't be cheap. Think of the long game and give real value. It has to be something that pattern interrupts and lets the potential customer forgo the fact they've never heard of you before.

When it comes to Retargeting - offers are also ideally tied to the particular page your website visitor was on. As mentioned previously, it's a lot easier to sell:

- Nike Air Max 90, black.
- Garage conversions.
- Pension plans for 30 year olds.

…to the person who was just looking at that page, rather than sending them an ad for:

- Here's our footwear store.
- Here's our General Builder homepage.
- John Smith IFA.

Your **audience** needs to be carefully defined. Who do you want to target? Who are your best customers? Do the guys that buy your Harley's also watch Sons of Anarchy or are they mostly accountants? Do you want to only sell to those within a 2-mile radius of you? Can you target the entire English speaking world? It's important to build a customer profile because the more accurate you are in your targeting the better results you'll get.

If you only have an outline, then you can learn it in a few different ways:

- If you're using ads to quite general cold audiences, you can look through the analytics and build it from there based on what demographics are taking the most interest to make your audience type more accurate.

- You can send ads to people that like specific pages (like in the Teespring example with sports teams). So if someone *'Likes'* yoga (as in they've liked the page or listed it as a hobby), or a specific TV show, or even one of your competitors' pages – you can send ads to those people because they fit your offline demographic (or if you just want to encourage potential customers away from your competition). If you're a masseuse or in physical therapy, you could target users that have liked *'sciatica relief'* pages. If you're a hypnotherapist you can target the likers of *'stop smoking'* pages. If you're a jeweller, you can target people with *'engaged'* as their relationship status. If you only coach CEO's in Austin, Texas, then you can set that as your demographic.

- If you do Retargeting, as I mentioned you can build what's called a *'Lookalike Audience'* where Facebook, for example will say *"OK, if these people in this demographic, in this area, with these interests are visiting the website, then these people with the same behaviour profile will also likely be interested"*. This is extremely helpful. Put a bit of code you might never need use on your website but 6 months later if you decide to run ads you've got a lookalike audience based on who's been visiting your website.

In terms of cost, the landscape will change rapidly and frequently. A few examples: Just now LinkedIn is expensive (but remember the KPI section – more expensive leads might mean better, higher paying clients), Facebook is pretty middle of the road - depending on the ad type, Instagram ads both *'post'* and *'story'* are cheap (and since Facebook owns Instagram you can manage the ads on there with your Facebook ones) and YouTube video ads are also very cheap for what they are.

There are also different types of adverts within each platform. Some are links out of the platform and on to your website. Some are messenger ads – meaning when an ad is clicked it opens up a messenger conversation, which is more intimate, rather than a link that takes you out of the platform. Some are Click-To-Call where the lead immediately phones you. There are many others, depending on the platform and the more advanced strategies are typically more expensive; but research what types work for others in your industry, test it all yourself and garner your own data.

All will get more expensive. Social media, particularly the ads, are in their infancy. **The Internet** is still in its infancy, never mind anything else. More new starts and more traditional companies and corporations are moving in. The more they see the return being better on social media because that's where the eyes are – the more they'll shift their budget over to it, thus pushing the price up for everyone else.

Make hay while the sun shines on social ads.

Don't worry. First it was print, then radio, then TV, then the internet, then Google, then the current social media crop. The landscape is constantly evolving, with new mediums coming out all of the time. There will be plenty to jump on if this ever dries up. Marketers adapt and you can follow their success.

When using social media, particularly ads - only use automation if you need it. Automation makes our lives easier, but all of my personal experience shows that people want human interaction. It seems a bit odd that some people prefer to message behind screen in order to avoid actually having to communicate verbally with a real, live person …but for some reason they draw the line at talking to a robot, even when they choose that method of communication. Some like the convenience but still want a human.

Automation takes a few different forms on social media. The two main ones are auto- responses as soon as someone makes contact - the other is more commonly known as *'Messenger Bots'* that follow a sequence with a user.

The first one looks a bit like:

"Thanks for getting in touch with ABC Plumbers, you can call us on… or email us at... If it's a technical enquiry… If it's a complaint…"

You get the idea. It can be very insincere – especially if it doesn't fit within the rigid parameters of what the message covers, and it turns people off.

Turn any auto responses off. They are disingenuous. They only serve you when you're in the middle ground of truly having too many messages to handle but can't justify taking on an additional member of staff. From my own clients' point of view, they either have their own member of staff, or I have my assistant do it. No messages getting left unreplied to and no substitution for human contact for the potential customer.

Bots are a little more sophisticated. Ranging from multiple choice questions that take users down a path to the result they want – to *'reading'* what the user has typed and predicting an answer based on the words contained in the original message. Something like:

Hi <name>, how can we help you today?
- Reserve a table.
- **Book an event.**
- See today's lunch menu.
- See today's dinner menu.
- Make a complaint.

Thank you. What kind of event would you like to book?
- Kids birthday party.
- Wedding.
- Corporate event.

…or the user messages to say *"I wish to make a complaint about my dining experience last night!"* - The bot reads the word *'complaint'* and sends a link to the complaint form. This might be fine if the bot gets it right, but having run many ads for many clients – many responses are so nuanced that using a robot can either get it wrong or not give a full, specific answer the customer might need – or indeed deserve.

Only use bots if you get so much volume you cannot manage it. Most businesses operate during certain hours and handling things that come through out-with them can either wait until opening or be dealt with at the time on a case by case basis. Most businesses aren't getting the kind of volume that can't be managed by the owner if it's a small business or a designated member of staff.

Bots should be a last resort to solve a big problem and shouldn't replace human interaction out of apathy or lazy management. Fewer instances will see the user impressed at the supposed *'slick operating process'* than the user appreciating some personal feedback. If you can afford ads and you're genuinely too busy to reply yourself – get someone else to do it. Only use bots as a last resort where the traffic is just too huge, or you really feel the *'slick'* process will impress your users more.

If my client can't devote time to it themselves or can't put a member of staff on it – I'll always suggest putting my assistant on it so she can answer with what would be the most common replies, but answer more specifically. If anything came up that she's not comfortable answering accurately she'll message or phone the client.

Be sure to segment user responses in the back end. Mark them as complete, flag them for another admin and so on. You can win sales you wouldn't have otherwise got had you not organised your social messaging and responses better. You can also retain existing customers or better encourage them to buy again if it's on point.

As I say; be willing to spend and lose the money, have no expectations. Start small with your budget and grow out – adjusting images, copy, offer and audience gradually. Use retargeting and lookalike audiences. Test different ad types across the different platforms and don't use automation unless you have to, or unless you're sure your audience will like it.

Remember that the market never lies. If it's not working, it's nothing personal. Look at what works in your testing, look at what works with others in your industry, tweak it and give your audience what they want - not what you think they need.

Always be looking to do better. Never rely on it as your sole source of leads, because as I mentioned before, platforms can change their TOS at any time and demonetise you, shut your ad down or your audience can simply move on to the next big thing.

WEBINARS

This will be industry dependant, but learning how to build a funnel and lead potential clients into webinars can change how you do your marketing forever.

Webinars are live seminars that you watch online. Many viewers can join the channel from the comfort of their home or office with a computer, tablet or smartphone. They can take many forms, such as the host being directly visible and talking to the camera that everyone can see, or perhaps it's a screencast of a PowerPoint presentation, or witnessing a conference call or group interview with multiple hosts, or even demonstrating a product. If it's a smaller, more intimate webinar – you might even be visible, but typically it's a one-to-many type of set up.

Again, typically the format is around delivering a lot of value and then ending with a sales pitch. The best ones I've ever seen give 90% of their advice or content away for free on the call; building goodwill, establishing yourself as an authority, offering a Q&A and then the *'sell'* at the end is what ties it all together or makes the whole thing you've taught them to do themselves easier.

Think of my client Paul's example, which I gave earlier. Instead of trying to get one customer at a time, you find a way to promote to many at once. Webinars are what Paul does, visiting companies and giving a presentation to multiple employees, but without even having to leave the office. Along the lines of *"Here's how you can improve your fitness and health while living a busy life"* – he gives loads of value and the employees never need take him on as their personal trainer, but if they did, he would be able to give them personal tuition and hold them accountable.

When it's online it's also much easier to get clients into your funnel. When they've finished watching your webinar, your product could be a small commitment, even as low as say £9 to build trust. Then, if they buy that and see they don't get stung you can immediately move into an up-sell for significantly more. You could go the other way and start with a large offer, which most typically reject which moves them into a down-sell that seems a lot less risk.

This can get very deep, for example:

- Low offer.
- Viewer buys.
- High offer.
- Viewer rejects.
- Medium compromise offer.
- Viewer still rejects.
- Medium low offer.

I'm not a massive fan of this sort of thing, but it's a proven model. It's more to illustrate that as with anything in this section, you can go as deep as you like with a plethora of webinar platforms that can offer all of these types of sales back ends.

When you market to potential clients, have them enter your funnel by offering a webinar instead of an eBook or similar. Give value on the webinar while sitting in your home or office - you can even record it beforehand if you've got too much anxiety about doing it live, take questions at the end and up-sell your services.

You could even run it as a paid for programme with regular *'shows'*.

You can invite your existing email lists or potential clients to join. You could run social ads inviting leads onto it or you could ask your clients or business friends who they know that might like to come on and learn. You could use Facebook and LinkedIn groups your part of to invite members. That one is especially good if you've already built up a good reputation on those groups as an authority and value giver.

You can also record the webinar live then offer it to those that never made it on to the live call. You now have a permanent asset to use as a value giver or sales tool forever, or as long as the content is relevant. You can repurpose this to your social media, or as an opt-in itself, as a blog post, or put it on your podcast ...and so on.

Also, take note, as from the YouTube video section – audio is most important; but remember the whole thing is a representation of your business. It should be smart, helpful, well prepared and professional – just like you (professional as in good – it doesn't have to be wooden).

Remember, as I keep saying, learn the lessons from running your business about what your customers **really** want. If you can prove beforehand that you'll solve a genuine pain point and all they have to do is turn up at a screen at a particular time – they will be there!

PODCASTS

We've gone backwards.

We seemed to be on this upward trajectory where first there was hand writing, then the printed word, then radio, then TV, then the internet, then virtual reality. Each getting more visual and involving more of the senses each time.

Now we're back at just audio.

Podcasts aren't new – I used to listen to them in the car on the way to and from work back in the day. I still listen to them now. Over half the population have listened to a podcast at some point in their life, but less than 10% listen to them on a regular basis. Yet there were half a million active podcast channels in 2018 and just 1 year later there are an additional 200,000. In 2018 there were 18 million episodes and now there are 29 million! That's a crazy jump in frequency.

So why are we back at audio only? First of all, it takes an absurd amount of time for the public to adopt something and have it go mainstream. Look at the growth mentioned above and that's with less than 10% of the population listening regularly – how lucrative (and essential) will it be to have your voice out there as this grows? Get a run on this now so you have an established channel when there's 5x as many people listening to podcasts.

Growth is partly down to the introduction of Alexa. So, who is Alexa?

"Alexa, play the latest 'Joe Rogan Experience' podcast."

Alexa is Amazon's digital assistant. A device called an Echo which sits in your home or office (anywhere with a power supply and an internet connection really) that plays audio, but more importantly – responds to voice commands. You can have Alexa:

- Play a song, album or artist you like.

- Give you the weather.
- Tell you a joke.
- Announce the current score line in your favourite sport.
- Add an item to your shopping list or order a product.
- Dim your lights.
- …launch a podcast you like!

Amazon's Echo is probably the most famous, but the likes of Google (Home) and Apple (HomePod) have their own versions.

The growth of these devices has meant many people are getting into audio again while they do things around the house. Work, cook, chill – audio can be running in the background just by verbally commanding it.

Similarly, the rise in paid music subscriptions like Spotify, Apple Music, Google Play and YouTube Music now offer podcasts instead of just music. This means regardless of where you are; at home, in the office, in the car or on the bus - you can be listening and be entertained or learning.

Podcasts are internet audio shows that anyone with a microphone and an internet connection can set up. The best ones have a purpose, a theme and target a specific audience.

As with everything you do in marketing, you must ask:

What's in it for them?

This is not a platform for your stream of consciousness, unless you're incredibly profound and listeners will actually gain massively from hearing your ramblings. All of us non-Gandhi's will need a structure and clear understanding of what value our channel gives. That could be anything from business advice to comedy.

You **could** just talk, but most shows follow a format of having some sort of expert guest, where questions are asked either regimented or with a degree of flow. Others review things, others tell a story, like having a book read to you.

Start with a foundation you want to set in terms of topic, then use tools like Google Trends and Buzzsumo to find out what's trending in that niche, which will help you pick your topic titles. The amount of people searching for a particular topic will give you a good barometer of how accurately you will be servicing your audience's needs. The better you do this, the more popular your podcast channel will be.

As I've mentioned before – audio is most important in videos. This is audio only, so it **must** be excellent. The standard is rightly high in the podcast medium so make sure yours is on par. The great news is that it doesn't take a huge investment to have that – so don't be intimidated by it.

205

You can get an excellent USB microphone for £100, ones that just plug in to your PC or laptop and can also record 2 way conversations if you're planning on doing interviews (you can also record your interviews over skype or similar – they don't need to be in person). I've even seen podcasters use mics that cost half that! Then it's just down to finding a quiet place to record with the least amount of background noise. You can record using a free software like Audacity and do some quick editing to clean up background noise (very simple - YouTube it) then it's just a case of adding your intro and outro (if you have them).

Intros (and possibly an outro) are good ways to make your podcast more professional. A jingle that sets the tone for what type of podcast you have, along with either you or someone you've hired to voice over. For clients I've used jingles purchased on AudioJungle - but there will be many others you could Google, and for the voiceover I've used both Fiverr and hired a person in real life (in fact, Fiverr can do the whole thing if you don't fancy stitching the two together).

To launch your podcast to the masses I recommend having, say, 3 episodes to start with rather than 1. This can give a better idea of the topics you'll cover once people start viewing the channel. If they only see 1 episode it gives less context about the direction the channel is going.

You could just launch on iTunes (the most popular) if you want, but there are multiple platforms available with different levels of reach. A good way to manage this (if you want to take your channel seriously) is to sign up to a podcast distribution tool where you only need to upload your episode and descriptions once and it posts that podcast across all your accounts, along with distributing the promotion of it across your social platforms and website. These distribution tools have useful analytics to track your channels success as well as built-in monetisation options.

To get a good start and build momentum, ask your friends, family, email list, clients and so on to:

- Visit your channel.
- Download / listen to the 3 episodes you've launched with.
- Subscribe to your channel.
- Leave a review.

This shows the different platforms, like iTunes, that your podcast is worth listening to, which will help you move up in their popularity charts.

You could run a competition when you first launch (with the prize being industry / subject matter relevant) to encourage distribution and maybe do some paid social media ads to get the reach further out of just your own contact sphere.

Try and keep to a schedule. People like routine, it shows professionalism and it helps with your own discipline, so you don't put it off. When distributing, it could be a good idea to, say, launch each episode using the distribution tool on the first day, then stagger the rest of the announcements over the likes of social media, email and so on throughout the week so you're getting a nicer curve in engagement instead of the 1-day spike from the day it was launched. This shows the platforms that your traffic is more consistent, and you're being more consistently listened to.

So, once you're up and running:

- Keep your posting consistent.
- Work on priming the pump for your future topics and interviews.
- Make your titles and descriptions really helpful and relevant to what's discussed in each episode, the benefits to the listener and outside links to useful resources.
- Keep visitors on your channel by mentioning and linking to previous podcasts of yours.
- Tee up future episodes by mentioning what you'll be talking about next or in the future.

Do all of this and, as I've said, prepare for the growth in the medium. Podcasts have been around for a long time but with only 10% of the population regularly using them it shows that major growth in the industry is still to happen. Get in there with good quality content, so when the majority of the public finally adopt it with the help of the new voice activated hardware and software, you're already established.

COLLABORATION

This is huge, and also hugely underutilised. If you are an electrician – it's good to be friends with builders. Builders get work - builders need electricians. You're a photographer? Build relationships with wedding planners. You're a removal company? Give commissions to estate and letting agents.

Many of these should often go without saying, but there's creative ways to do it both online and offline.

Remember I mentioned how my fitness client, Paul gives free talks to company employees on how to improve their Health & Fitness and with no hard sell - some of those employees become clients? That is not an obvious link …at all. My other fitness client, Nadia, sells her online fitness course to companies for their employees, creating multiple sign-ups for a group discount. Again, not an obvious link at all (but very creative).

Really think about how, instead of getting one-to-one sales at a time, you can get one-to-many sales.

In more traditional media in general, like TV, film and music, people have collaborated for years and for far more lucrative reasons than just wanting to work with someone else that they admire, respect, idolise or *'have always wanted to work with'*.

First of all, there's the reputation and authority increase of having worked with that person or people. Then there's leveraging each other's audience across different platforms: If person A has 1 million devoted fans and person B has the same; a collaboration introduces the fans of person A to person B, then some of those fans become person B's fans, and vice-versa.

This is the same with internet celebrities or even general business owners. If both you and the other collaborator(s) have audiences, is it worth each of you being introduced to the other's audience through a collaboration? That could be a podcast interview, a YouTube video, or it could be an online course or project you both start.

When building these connections, establishing yourself and your company or brand as an authority, you often begin to carve out a group of you as experts or thought leaders in a subject, discipline or niche. You'll find more and more people will look to involve or interview you in your industry and, best of all, your action and efforts in and around your collaboration group will make you better at what you do.

You can also pool your budgets and resources like premises or connections or expenses; to go after more worthwhile or lucrative ventures in your space, or indeed elsewhere.

When this happens, you and your group of collaborators can even become trailblazers in where your subject matter, discipline, industry or niche goes next.

COPYWRITING

As I mentioned in the first section: I read 6 books in 2016 on Direct Response Copywriting alone, because I knew it was something that was massively missing from my toolset. I also sought-out the mentorship of a master copywriter, who I met when I was in Chiang Mai, to hone my skills and fast-track my early sales pages.

I could type marketing agency speak all day, in my sleep, like a stream of consciousness that would barely need any tweaking, but…

This was completely different.

It's not the kind of writing to pass an English exam, it's not like writing a book, it's not like journalism, it's not like the writing you learn in any kind of state education system. Considering them similar is like saying it's the same as sketch drawing – because both use a pencil.

Have you ever been on those long-form sales pages? Long-form as they seem to go on forever. The text is usually quite narrow on the page with a story:

- There's a bunch of claims in a catchy headline.
- Bullet points.
- Money back guarantees.
- Bonus offers.
- Testimonials or case studies.
- Big calls to action – often with a discount and a time limit.

That's Direct Response Copywriting. They might be long, not because they waffle (in fact, they shouldn't waste an inch) – but they give **so much** useful information all the while pushing your *"I must have this"* button.

…and it works. The difference it made to my clients was stark.

The whole point of a sales letter is to articulate exactly what makes your product unique and prove you can solve a problem better than your competition. It can often take me weeks of talking to a client and researching the industry to really get what that angle is. The client is so entrenched in their business that their uniqueness is simply second nature to them. It's how they do things. It might be the way they've always done things.

Some might fear putting out the kind of copy that makes people take notice. It doesn't look like what everyone else is doing.

These business owners should decide what's more important to them.

However, with great power comes great responsibility – it's so effective that it can be used to sell garbage - so only use this theory and these strategies if you genuinely have a product or service that solves a genuine need.

Don't be boring. Anyone can type boring. Any agency worth their salt can write that generic shit. It doesn't sell a damn thing. No agency fluff - just what works. Most agencies will produce fancy imagery with typical slogans and copy, to the point it's all hipster self-indulgence. What looks good in a graphic design degree is completely irrelevant to what makes people buy. Study human behaviour and the art of persuasion. What **actually** works, rather than being the victim of an expensive and glossy centerpiece used in a Starbucks drinker's portfolio.

Be brave, be bold. Don't be a dick, don't write cheques your ass can't cash, don't be disingenuous, don't use smoke and mirrors, but above everything – don't be afraid to tell everyone what you're genuinely good at.

Copywriting is arguably the most important part of the whole marketing process. In this industry you always have to be studying and learning what works. Regardless of how good I thought I was at copy at the start of 2016, I quickly realised if I wanted to make the biggest improvement to my clients' results, this is where I would focus most of my study attention.

Understanding what really works, what makes potential customers become your actual customers - is rarely what you think it is and has nothing to do with what you think that **you personally** would respond to. There's a structure and theories that you have to constantly hone to get the right message, at the right time, to the right people in order to convert.

The right copy just works.

This is why so many business owners try their hand at say, for example, Facebook ads and give up after one or two tries, thereby throwing money away. If you're going to do this on your own, then learn Direct Response Copywriting.

It's called Direct Response because it's designed to get a result then and there:

- A sale.
- A sales call.
- A newsletter sign-up.
- An event booking.
- Downloading your opt-in.

...and so on.

Its roots go much further back, but the style as we know it was founded, created, theorised or whatever you want to call it, around the 1950's. If you've ever seen the TV show Mad Men, then this captures the time perfectly (there's also some excellent examples of Direct Response Copywriting in that show, but I digress).

Almost everything you read on Direct Response Copywriting mentions David Ogilvy as its godfather. He had some of the biggest brands as clients at his agency in the 50's. Arguably his most famous ad was for Rolls Royce in the late 50's, to which the headline read:

"At 60 miles an hour, the loudest noise in this new Rolls-Royce comes from the electric clock."

Sales went up 50% the following year.

Amazingly, with everything that's changed in the world since then, about how we consume information, and the sheer volume of it – Direct Response Copywriting is unchanged. Which is why it's so important to take heed with what I said at the start of this section: Mediums come and go, but understanding the fundamental principles of what makes people buy will never change – you only need to take what you already know and adapt it to that medium.

"People will do anything to relieve their anxiety."
- Dr Arnold Rosen, Mad Men

Your sales page should articulate that you solve that anxiety, and better than anyone else. You should describe the readers' problems even better than they could. If you can do that you will prove that you **get it**; and if you understand it (or can articulate it) even better than them - then when you say you have the solution they think that you must genuinely have it:

*"They totally **get** me!"*

A great sales page will tell a story, either literally a story - or a romance about the product or service and it will solve a need.

To veer off slightly - almost every Hollywood movie can be broken down into 2 journeys...

The first journey is accomplishment:

- The character (the stories' hero).
- That character's desire for a goal.
- The conflict involved in achieving the goal.
- Then achieving the goal …or not, because…

The second journey (running parallel with the first) is their transformation in becoming a different person:

- The person they were before and their negative beliefs (usually about themselves).
- The person they've become and realising those beliefs are false, either after reaching the goal or realising they didn't actually need that goal in the first place (the latter not so relevant when you're selling a product or service!).

Think about **any** movie – it almost always ties in.

Anyway, this is important in direct response because it is the perfect formula for a story …and stories sell. Remember I said the key is to get the person reading the sales page in the shoes of the person you're telling the story about. This is why getting your targeting right and your sales page in front of the right people is so important:

"That person in the story is just like me… They have the same goals as me… Wait, this product helps me reach that same goal as it did for them? Shut up and take my money!"

It really is as simple as that. That's why I bang on about case studies, they're real and if you tell the story just right, as well as getting that story in front of the right people, you'll get sales.

People are crying out to be sold to. They want to buy. They want that rush they get from reading your copy, telling themselves they're going to buy, then actually pulling the trigger. You know that your product or service works, so make sure when they do that it has the desired effect, making the buying choice a good one that reinforces their decision. If it does - they'll buy again, and they'll spend more when they do.

Some of the main reasons people buy:

- Fear (like the fear of losing out).
- Love.
- Greed.
- Envy.

- Guilt.
- Pride.
- Shame.

Blair Warren takes credit for the now famous (in copywriting circles at least) sentence from his One Sentence Persuasion Course essay that says:

> *"People will do anything for those who encourage their dreams, justify their failures, allay their fears, confirm their suspicions and help them throw rocks at their enemies."*

- Encouraging their dreams makes the reader feel that what they want is possible with your product or service.

- Justifying their failures makes the reader feel like they aren't responsible for their own failings, which people **love**.

- Allaying their fears makes the reader feel like they are being listened to, that their fears make sense …but relax - you're going to solve them.

- Confirming their suspicions makes the reader feel like they already knew something all along about how things are – that you understand it's a genuine concern, but your product or service helps them get around it.

- Helping someone throw rocks at their enemies makes the reader feel like you're in it together – you're side by side with them, or ready to catch them if they fall. It's the only time the word *"We"* should be used in your copy, as in *"Us, together"*. It's never about you, it's about the reader.

…and while we're on the subject of which words to use, I particularly love:

- You.
- Deserve.
- Because.

No, not necessarily together (*"**You deserve** this product **because**…"*), but individually they have so much power.

"You" should be the foundation of your copy. As I just said; it's about the reader, not you. Mentioning *"you"* as often as possible (as long as it makes complete sense in the sentence) shows the reader that you're speaking to them directly. Like there's no one else in the room. It is like you created the page and wrote out your copy especially for them. Again, the only time to use *"we"* is when it's you and the reader teaming up to throw rocks at their enemies i.e. *"We're going to…"*

The word *"deserve"* just works. People like to be told they deserve things. It makes them feel like it's ok to want something and renders if they actually do indeed deserve it or not meaningless because you've given them a pass. Now that I've mentioned it, you'll start to see *"deserve"* written quite often in the marketing of products.

"Because" is a great word …because studies in real life environments have shown when you use it – whatever follows is more likely to be believed. If you make a statement – use *"because"* after the statement and before the explanation to make the reader respond far more willingly.

Those are a few of my favorites, but you can find comprehensive lists of words that have great impact by consuming more Direct Response Copyrighting content all over the web.

Write like you talk and speak the readers' language.

I write like I talk. This book is not written in Direct Response, but it's written mostly like I talk (hopefully you're reading it in a Glaswegian accent, too). This is another reason why Direct Response in nothing like traditional forms of writing. Write how you speak, like you're having a real conversation. People respect the honesty of it, and it relaxes them. I write like I talk because it's the easiest way to articulate that what I'm saying is intended. It's an insight into how I say things and befriends the reader. It's honest.

We've covered this earlier but it's really important to mirror the language of your audience. The terms and expressions they use in or about your industry, and stories or phrases they can relate to - because they might not be the same as yours:

*"Don't be a **Nerf Herder!** Get our new and incredibly fast quad-core i7 system!"*

*"Get rid of your **Chicken Strips** by investing in our unrivalled Knee Down riding course today!"*

*"The office is now running **smoother than the team's morning latte's**"*

You might not know what a Nerf Herder is (a Star Wars insult) when selling PC parts to gamers, or what Chicken Strips (the outside edge of a tyre that often gets unused due to lack of lean angle) are to bikers - but the audience does, and that's what matters. You've personalised your product to them.

You're looking to tap into your readers' true desires that are based on the real emotions (like fear, greed, love and envy mentioned previously) that make people buy, and using their language while you do it.

What copywriting should not be:

As I mentioned, copywriting is powerful and should only be used to promote good products or services. To encourage the right people to find the right product or service that will genuinely improve their life. Copywriting should not be used to sell garbage or turd-polish. There are real people at the other side of the screen, parting with real money. Just like starting a business – you have a responsibility to create a good product and service that doesn't need to sell snake oil to survive.

Copywriting is also not clickbait, well it is – but it shouldn't be! Clickbait is usually what's now been coined as Fake News. Where the article bears virtually no resemblance to the title. How do you feel when you read an article and the title is so deliberately misleading?

It's disgusting and disingenuous to the journalistic profession.

It might be the title of a politically motivated piece that hopes you only read that title to form an opinion about something - but when you read the article you can clearly see *"that's not what that person actually said"*, or later you'll see the whole interview or action on video and see what you read was deliberately taken out of context to suit an agenda.

With product or service marketing you will see the same – don't be that person. As you get better at copywriting, use your powers for good. Use it to get a genuinely good product or helpful service into the possession of readers that genuinely need it.

So how do you break down a sales page? This will vary wildly depending on the product but the difference between hokey-garbage and genius-earner can be a fine one.

Keep the page simple, mostly black text on a white background and only use images if they're helpful. Not to *'break up'* the text, not to make it look more *'professional'* or *'classy'*. Images only help if they're displaying something the text is saying. The text box will typically be narrower, rather than edge to edge like a normal webpage.

Start by saying you can make their problem go away and explain how your product or service does that. Show proof that it works. You do not want generic copy that your competition is using – make it stand out. Again, this is why real case studies are so good – they're unique to you.

You should only care about what the potential customer reading the sales page wants, not what you want to sell them. Test, test and test again, always giving them what they want.

A good framework for creating any sales page, particularly your first few, is to follow AIDA:

- **Attention:** This is done through the headline, the image in the ad or at the top of the page, and the initial copy. It should be gripping, bold and solve a problem.

- **Interest:** This is the story that has continuity with the initial *'attention'* that solves the problem – this can be in first person but is often spoken indirectly.

- **Desire:** This is where you list the benefits, but that doesn't make people buy - so provide proof, typically in the form of credentials and testimonials. Hammer home how your product is guaranteed to solve their problem. Make the reader desire it!

- **Action**: Handle any objections and then make the offer. Do not do it meekly. You've stated your claim and you've backed it up – it's time for the reader to buy. Scarcity, guarantees, sometimes extras and adding more than one bonus helps.

Everything begins with the headline. Like the Rolls-Royce one earlier – it's incredibly powerful and important. It's the attention grabber that sets the tone for the rest of the ad. As Mr Ogilvy said himself:

"80 cents of your dollar should be spent on writing headlines."

He learned through testing that 4 out of 5 people read the headline before anything else, and that 5 times as many people read the headline over the body copy - which is the reason for the above quote.

The headline must be a pattern interrupt - something that makes a reader stop scrolling and say:

"What?"

Your whole job with the rest of the copy is to now back up whatever you've said that made them stop. Remember - No fake news! So, while it makes them stop - it still has to be real.

If you can't make them stop with a claim about how your product or service is better in some way, while still being truthful:

Congratulations: You've got a generic …at best, business.

I'll let you into a secret. Most of my clients either didn't know what it was that made them unique or better - or they just didn't know how to frame it right. You might have read that headline above and thought: *"fuck, my business is generic, and he's just hit the nail on the head"*, I've probably not – it's more likely you're too close to it. It can take a bit of dissecting or soul searching to get it, then you trade off it. The best bit about that is there's no shame in it, because it's what you're supposed to do in your business – explain why you are different or better. It's not snake oil if it's true and you should be proud to talk about it!

So, back to the headline and sub-headline: Make the reader feel like their prayers will be answered, their anxieties eliminated, their friends jealous or any of the other primal desires and reasons people buy. Make them truly feel how utterly unmissable your product or service would be, and how great purchasing, owning or experiencing it will be. Yes, just with the headline and sub-headline. How do they benefit?

I won't use clients for an example, given they paid for their campaigns and won't want them plagiarised. A very similar example to one of my most profitable client campaigns would be (names changed and using my own industry as an example):

"Look At How David, A 42 Year Old Drop-Out From Glasgow With No Qualifications & Over £24,000 In Debt, Built His Business, Quit His Job And Is Now Debt Free! ...and how you too can see results in as little as a few weeks with a business and marketing strategy from an award winning business coach, who has worked with the likes of Howden Global, Rolls-Royce & Aston Martin

How one to one personal coaching, support and advice transformed David's vision and confidence into a profitable business that supports his family."

That first paragraph in its entirety is the headline, the sub-headline is the single sentence below it. Lengths of both can vary wildly – this is just an example.

The only reason this can go out is if the wording is truthful.

- *"Look"* is a command, provoking a reaction to see the case study for themselves.

- It gives specifics. A name to the person and numbers; like age, location and debt amount.

- It explains how David did it.

- It gives the reader a realistic time frame.

- It tells them the brief steps on how they'll do it, creating intrigue.

- The business coach gives social proof and credibility; given that they are award winning and have worked with some of the biggest names.

- It helps the reader throw rocks at their enemies by proving all those who doubted them wrong. Maybe their classmates (*"drop out"*), colleagues (*"quit his job"*) or their partners / parents (*"supports his family"*).

Did you like that? Good. Did you read it in a cheesy 1980's American infomercial tone from a business coach with fake teeth? Great, because it works.

It might seem *'salesy'* but it's supposed to. It's supposed to be interesting. You think it turns people off? You want to get in the back door by pretending you don't want sales or that you'd finesse it better and more subtly than that? No. That headline **is** what you're doing – it's just being more honest about it.

That's how you grab attention with Direct Response Copywriting. You can turn the dial up or down on it depending on the industry, your audience and your comfortability.

That is just one example of a headline style, and there are many. It could also be picked apart and improved on - perhaps with more adjectives and compelling language, or including scarcity, or a time limit. It could be more topical, it could be even more specific, or the promise could be harder hitting. The great thing about it is that even the best copywriters often get predictions wrong about what will perform best - you've got to put it out there and let the market decide.

Your job, now that you have the reader's attention is to then break all of that down in the rest of the copy, telling the story and proving it all. Then testing, testing and more testing, adjusting all of it and improving.

After the headline(s), I typically tell the story, firstly in the case study's (in this case David's) own words. This will be a full breakdown of David's situation, much in the same way as the Case Study section:

- The Problem.
- The Solution.
- The Result.

It has to be emotive. They should talk about the pain in great detail. I'm not talking about information that should be private – I mean the real descriptive emotion about how it was a problem, how it held David back and what he felt. How he felt like everything was hopeless and there was nowhere to turn.

Then go into detail about the product and how it helps. This often includes a section about you. Maybe you were also in a similar situation to David and the reader, talk openly about what that was like, how they are just like you were and how this is exactly how you got out of it. Your product or service has to be the absolute solution to it all and how many others you've helped. Be honest, be vulnerable and readers will appreciate it.

Your *"Why"* is very important. It isn't a feature, like a USP:

"Buy your wine from us, because unlike other companies; we supply a bottle opener with every order!"

219

It's the very essence of what you do. This message is part of what makes people use one company over another. It defines the tone of your copy, your advertising and the way you encourage a buyer. When people believe your *"Why"*, they buy (I may have accidentally created a cheesy jingle there).

> *"People don't buy what you do; they buy why you do it."*
> - Simon Sinek

A few tips:

- Nobody likes to read huge paragraphs of text, break it up nicely and type like you talk. Use bullet points whenever you can – people love reading bullet points.

- Grammatically incorrect is irrelevant if it helps you tell the story better. Starting sentences with *'because'* and *'but'* is not important. Capitalising the first letter of every word in the title helps people take notice and read it …and so on.

- Give details about your industry or the subject matter, like latest news and statistics that prove you know what you're talking about and have your finger on the pulse.

- Talk about the result. People are paying for the result. Not *"We will help clear your debt!"*, what will clearing your debt actually mean? Where will you be able to go? What will you be able to do? How will you feel? How will your family and friends see you?

- Go into great detail about specifics parts of your product or service that help resolve certain parts that make up the bigger picture. Be specific, this isn't an ad in a newspaper or billboard - you have as much space as you need. If you get the page in front of the right audience - they will care about the specifics. Be specific, but don't be boring.

Then use testimonials. Show proof in the pudding from multiple demographics if possible. A mixture of text and video testimonials is ideal. Some people prefer to read, some prefer to watch videos (you can also have a video at the top that covers everything mentioned in the sales page for this reason), but even those that prefer to watch videos might not be in a position to play audio wherever they're looking at your sales page from.

Tell the reader that you won't just take anyone, or that your product isn't for everyone. Filter down so people understand this is niche, thus understanding you're not just trying to sell to anyone who'll part with their cash.

Then give a summary of everything you've just said that the reader gets, then tell them the offer. As I just said – be confident. Your product is good and worth the money – so ask for it. Rather than *"Purchase"* or *"Buy"* or *"Add To Cart"* – make it compelling or a command like *"Buy Now!"* or *"Sign Me Up!"* or *"Let Me In!"*.

When it comes to price point – it's largely a state of mind. Particularly if you're selling an information product or something you've uniquely created. How much you charge and what you're comfortable with is mostly in your own head.

The better your copy is – the less important the price is.

Again, direct response is easier when you have a good business or product. When you have a good offer. When you have a USP, or if your USP is simply doing what you do better than everyone else - marketing should be an addition to an already good business.

There are many effective ways you can add to the offer:

- Offer a discount, or you can say that the numerical value of the product is X but you're only selling it for Y.

- Add free bonus products you have as part of them buying the main product.

- Give some sort of guarantee, like your product or service will do exactly what you say it will do, or alternatively a money back guarantee – which massively limits their risk (comparatively, very few people ever take you up on a refund).

- Put a time limit on the offer, which creates scarcity and a fear of missing out. Tell the reader you only have so many slots if it's a service, or you will remove the offer and put it back up to full price if it's a product – and so on. Make sure this is truthful and you follow through on it.

All of these can massively help a reader that's teetering to fully commit and get over the line.

Then, after the offer, explain exactly the process of what happens next after they buy your product or service; where they'll be taken, what they'll be sent and so on. Make them feel great about the step by step of what will happen if they click to buy.

Finally - put in an FAQ. This is a must in order to answer questions, handle objections they already have or really just an opportunity to talk about something they haven't thought of so you can put them further at ease about how your product or service helps.

Direct Response Copywriting is a great barometer for your business. The better your product or service is – the easier the sales page is to write. It's easier to talk about how it helps, who it helps, what they say, why you sell it, how it's better than the competition and so on.

Your business for whatever reason might not lend itself to long form sales pages (very few don't though) but these principals relate to all of your copy – no matter how small.

Finally: You must practice the shit out of this.

It's almost impossible to be good at it straight out of the gate, but you will get better. It's an incredible skill to have. I love how every other aspect of modern marketing changes in terms of the platforms, the styles and all the advancements we humans make in getting the right products and services to the right people.

…but what makes people buy in terms of human behaviour has been unchanged in human history, and the way direct response delivers it has been unchanged for nearly 70 years. Only our platforms for delivering that message have gotten better, and they'll continue to get better.

The early adopters of those platforms will benefit hugely; like Google AdWords at the turn of the century, Facebook ads a few years ago and currently Instagram ads. It'll keep moving from platform to platform, always improving what gets people's attention – but the framework of what motivates people to buy and how you explain it to them will outlive us.

ONLINE COURSES

I touched on this in the business section, but it seems right to put it here after everything that's been said about marketing, as it all comes into play on how you build and sell it.

I mentioned leverage and how to add to your business while still trading time for money. You have a ceiling on how many hours there are in a day. The example was training many clients in a group class, charging less per client but making more per hour. This is just one example how to create leverage on your time, with the added bonus of it being cheaper for the client and also creating community.

I also mentioned the next stage, which is having your customers or clients **pay for the result**, rather than the numerical time it takes you to complete the task.

The final stage is passive income (actually, the final stage is investment - but I'm neither qualified nor have the experience to talk about that in any detail). This is no longer trading time for money. You create something - an asset like a book, a course or physically manufactured product that can be sold over and over again with no more work involved (except perhaps the odd thing; like tech support, if that's relevant – but they can all grow as you do).

You can create a course on ...well... just about anything - as has been proven. From sewing and knitting to forest survival, public speaking to pet training. This can be something you do as a profession or as a hobby.

Typically, all the information would be behind a pay-wall on a website. The user pays a one-time, annual or monthly fee to gain access.

There are a number of ways to do this. You can:

- Build the website yourself.
- Have someone build it for you.
- Pay a provider a monthly subscription to use their online course platform

that you can White Label (something that allows you to rebrand as if you made it).

- You can also submit your content to existing providers that have much more traffic, where you earn a commission when someone purchases your course on their platform, but you have no control - remember I mentioned previously about owning your own platform and not being at the mercy of someone else's. I would only do this if the momentum has completely died on your own website or if you don't have the time or the inclination to market it yourself.

Firstly, you need to decide:

- What it is you want to create and launch?
- What is your niche, and how niche do you want to go?
- What is your target demographic?
- Is it video, audio, text based or most likely a combination of all 3?
- Will it simply exist behind the pay-wall as information or will there be downloads, quizzes, exams to sit afterwards along with downloadable certifications? (all of which can be implemented in the software)
- Will you have an MVP (Minimum Viable Product) that you launch for a select group to get feedback before you launch to the masses with all the bells and whistles? If so, who will those people be and why?

You will need to break down exactly what the course entails and what sections you'll have. Will it go from start to finish like a book with chapters, where you move from lesson 1 to lesson 10; or will there be many different courses within your membership site where a member can pick and choose which ones to enrol in on the fly? Will you continue to add to the membership every month, constantly delivering new value in order to keep your users paying a subscription?

Like I say, everything I've mentioned previously in this book applies here:

The most important thing will be to listen to your users' feedback. Give them what they want. Learn, grow and adapt accordingly. Never wait until the thing is perfect – that's an excuse not to launch. Start with a *'thing'* and make the users make the thing better. You don't know what they'll say before you do it. Even if you start with the shittest thing – listening to your audience and adapting accordingly will guarantee you don't have a shit thing for long.

You then want to look at how you're going to promote the course. Again, everything you've read so far in this book comes into play here:

- What is your **Sales Funnel**?
- Do you have an **Opt In** to get someone interested in the course and their email address to build an email list and send an email sequence to?
- Will you create a **Webinar** to funnel viewers to your course?

- Will you have a dedicated **Sales Page** on your website, instead of just sending people to your course homepage and hoping they convert?
- What sort of **Retargeting** are you going to set up for those that visit your course website or sales page, but don't buy there and then?
- What **Social Media** platforms will you be on talking about your course and how will it differ on each platform? What images will you use on Instagram? How will you utilise video on YouTube? Will you set up a group on Facebook for your members?
- Will you have a **Social Ad** or **PPC** budget to reach out further?
- Can you garner **Testimonials** and **Case Studies** quickly from people you trust to try the course and give you honest feedback?
- Do you have an **SEO** strategy around how you word everything and what other websites you can promote on?
- Can you get guest spots on podcasts or be interviewed for other websites or news media, or **Guest Post** to promote your course?
- Will you create your own **Podcast** as a funnel?
- Can you **Collaborate** with people in your network to talk about your course?
- Will you offer a **Referral** or affiliate scheme to get more sign ups?
- Are you encouraging existing customers to **Recommend** their friends, family and colleagues?
- Is the course **Adaptable** to move with the times like I mentioned with VR?

You could also offer a Tripwire, which I touched on earlier. Basically, an offer that's much smaller than your main offer but builds confidence in the customer to buy the bigger offer. They think:

"I didn't get my fingers burned; the transaction was legit, and the content was worth it."

Meaning when it comes to upsell your offer, even if it's significantly more expensive - they're far more likely to purchase it having had a good experience. The barrier for them is subconscious mistrust, rather than the obvious conscious mistrust – so they subconsciously no longer consider it a barrier given they've parted with any amount of cash previously without being bitten or fleeced.

Your tripwire could be just about anything. Something the same as what you're offering as the full course, just a bite-size section. Then from there it's simple to transition to:

"Get the full course as well as… for only…".

Remember to build upsells into the overall course until you stop getting a lot of sales. Imagine you had huge sales of your course; more than you ever thought you would - only through hindsight you find out your buyers would've been happy to spend even more if you had another tier (or two!). That's a lot of money left on the table. You should be testing the spending limits of your audience – again, as long as you're genuinely providing exceptional value, not *"duping suckers"*. Once you stop getting upsell sales then you've reached your ceiling for that combination of either the quality of your product, your sales page effectiveness or the willing disposable income of your target market.

You can also upsell your own personal involvement, whether that be your skillset or mentorship.

Of course, accept this takes away from the passive income model in some way – but not necessarily a bad thing if that's what you want, prefer or enjoy. Your course might only be a supplementation of what you want your business to be.

Online Courses are the most effectively way to make passive income over the internet. Very few things are truly passive, so make sure you're constantly growing or improving your offering and also your marketing of your course. The sole goal of your course, much like your business, is to provide exceptional value - not to make money. If you provide exceptional value, the money will take care of itself.

TO FINISH THIS SECTION

Despite being longer than the first two sections combined - not having enough customers is a business problem, not a marketing problem. Marketing should supplement a good business, it shouldn't be snake oil that props it up. Marketing should be an addition to a business that is already successful at providing value to its customers.

It's vitally important to learn what works and do more of whatever that is. Start with a bit of intuition, but ultimately test everything. Be methodical with all paid ads in particular, otherwise you can burn through money unnecessarily.

You must build trust and authority, as well as marketing to your audience's chimp brain. People buy with emotion and justify it with logic.

You must learn how your audience speaks, for both copywriting and targeting those searching for you on google. You must be where your customers are.

You must retarget your audiences - people that have proven to be interested in your product, ensuring to cover the touch principal.

You must ask for referrals, testimonials and case studies.

You should build an email list or some form of customer data (ethically and legally) that you can always control, never leaving you at the mercy of any platform. You should have sales funnels across all your marketing efforts.

You should niche down, either entirely or in certain areas of your business in order to find the best clients willing to pay more for that specific niche.

You should be ready and willing to move into new arenas, to pioneer your industry on new platforms and technologies.

You should discover ways to future-proof your business and build passive income streams.

All of these will vary wildly from business to business, but it's important to take the ones relevant to you and make the conscious effort to implement them. Do it yourself or pay someone to do it. Remember; you can't have it both ways - you're either cash poor or time poor.

FINAL THOUGHTS

Hopefully, regardless of if you're just starting out or if you've been running a business for decades you found this book useful. Anything from some positive reinforcement to a complete reframe of your mind, how you run a business and how you market that business.

Starting a business and the subsequent years of difficulty and doubt has fundamentally changed me as a person, for the good. When I think back to when I was questioning even starting and all the early setbacks I had compared to who I am now - it scares me to think of never having taken that leap and it makes me extremely grateful for what I have now. For how comfortable things are and how all of it is down to the choices and sacrifices I made and storms I weathered.

I struggled many times, failed many times and it was all because of me. But as I mentioned earlier - that means the wins are also because of me.

Sometimes I wish I could go back and tell myself that it would all come good, because at times it was fucking horrible ...but who knows if that would've made me more complacent and less hungry?

If you'd told me 8 years ago that I'd be confident enough and have any sort of authority to write a book with the contents of this one I would have never believed you. This book never needs to become a best seller - simply the virtue of its existence gives me something that the keys to a new Ducati never would. All because I made a decision 8 years ago to stop mentally masturbating and to put my pride and my worth on the line.

The whole point of this book is to help others take less time than I did when starting out, or help those currently running a business. If I knew all of this at the start, things would have been a lot easier. Although the book goes into some details that will inevitably be outdated - the overall principals and fundamentals are evergreen.

I thought there would come a point where I'd be the finished article. But it's better than that...

You're never the finished article.

You get to keep going as long as you want, and you get better with every passing experience. It's a lifetime of growth and development that gets more rewarding the longer you're in it.

None of this book is taught in school because school, in its current form, is outdated. The system wants everyone in a box, and the best way to do that is to shoehorn everyone into a production line that stifles creativity and uniqueness.

We have enough bricks in the wall.

It's important we train the next generation about entrepreneurship, to at least offer it as a choice. We need less ambiguity about what an entrepreneur is or what a business owner does. It's not reserved for 3-piece suits, big boardrooms and fountain pens. It's not reserved for the wicked-smart that give keynotes wearing a hoodie, a beanie and a pair of Vans.

It can be for anyone that wants it. It's for anyone who's willing to work, to sacrifice, to struggle, to overcome. It's for anyone who's willing to put up with any initial bullshit until they no longer have to. It's for anyone who rejects drama, office politics and social norms. It's for anyone who refuses to accept that they can't do something based on their lack of privilege.

It's about the journey and it's not about the wins once you've made it that make you a winner - it's the struggles you overcame on the way.

It's about teaching the next generation the importance of providing value and not feeling special or entitled, regardless if they want to become a business owner or an employee.

A few years ago, I took a few days out of my working week to train young people, and it was the most rewarding thing I ever did - you could not come close to putting any sort of price on it. Ever since then my big picture was to help as many people as possible with my knowledge. Nothing feels better than someone thanking you for your support or sending you an email after they've listened to a podcast that you were a guest on, saying you inspired them to take action or change something.

Most of all we need to teach that being happy is the most important thing. Having time is the most important thing. Having peace of mind is the most important thing. Your mental health is the most important thing. Business and money are not as important as any of these things, it can only be a vehicle to help with them.

"Nothing is either good or bad, but thinking makes it so."
- Abraham Lincoln

It's important to understand that how you deal in your business day to day and how you approach situations, build your processes and market yourself is a state of mind. You can let your business stress you out or you can use it to make your life better - otherwise what was the point in starting in the first place?

Everything I ever stressed about either never happened, wasn't detrimental like I feared or simply never ended up anywhere near as bad as I thought. Any time I've faced my business problems and worries head on - they've went away. Each made me happier and a better person (and businessman) for it.

What should you do next?

What is the most popular story in history? Someone who doesn't have it, but wants it. What's *'It'*? ...well that's up to you to define. Whatever it is - I want to help you get it. Remember:

"We depend on other people's dreams coming true."
- Barbara Sher

Don't let this book be another piece of content that you consume but change nothing. Resist the urge to segue into something else. Get brilliant at what you're currently doing. You're on a current road, but it's getting too real and you need the escapism of something else. Those endorphins you've got for the new thing? You once had them for the thing you're doing now. Get out of this pattern, otherwise you'll keep moving from idea to idea and never get any reward other than the mental masturbation cycle you're stuck in.

Starting and running a business is truly one of the bravest things you can do and is unbelievably character building. It's opened up my life to some of the best experiences with some of the coolest people I've ever met. You will meet plenty of dickheads along the way, but they won't matter because the business will be **your** creation and part of **your** life. You decide who you let in.

Listen to the market and your audience, not generic people. Understand and provide real value. Build trust and authority. Persevere and refine. Reject *"Luck"*, any sort of magic and victim complexes. Find your people and collaborate. Set goals. Take action and risks. Educate yourself. Ask for referrals and testimonials. Be a producer, not a consumer. Be authentic and have integrity. Value time over money.

If you enjoyed this book or found it helpful, I'd love to hear from you. You can contact me at: info@graeme-lawson.com

Printed in Great
Britain
by Amazon